SURVIVING

SQUID

GAME

SURVIVING

SQUID

GAME

○ △ □

A GUIDE TO K-DRAMA, NETFLIX, AND GLOBAL

STREAMING

WARS

SUK-YOUNG KIM

APPLAUSE
THEATRE & CINEMA BOOKS

ESSEX, CONNECTICUT

APPLAUSE
THEATRE & CINEMA BOOKS

An imprint of Globe Pequot, the trade division of
The Rowman & Littlefield Publishing Group, Inc.
4501 Forbes Blvd., Ste. 200
Lanham, MD 20706
www.rowman.com

Distributed by NATIONAL BOOK NETWORK

Library of Congress Cataloging-in-Publication Data

Names: Kim, Suk-Young, 1970– author.
Title: Surviving Squid Game : a guide to K-drama, Netflix, and global
  streaming wars / Suk-Young Kim.
Description: Essex, Connecticut : Applause Press, 2023. | Includes
  bibliographical references.
Identifiers: LCCN 2022042737 (print) | LCCN 2022042738 (ebook)
  | ISBN
  9781493072729 (paperback) | ISBN 9781493072736 (epub)
Subjects: LCSH: Squid Game (Television program) | Television
  programs—Korea (South)—History. | Popular culture—Korea
  (South)—History—21st century. | Netflix (Firm) | Streaming
  video—Social aspects—Korea (South)
Classification: LCC PN1992.77.S683 K56 2023 (print) | LCC
  PN1992.77.S683
  (ebook) | DDC 791.45/72—dc23/eng/20221208
LC record available at https://lccn.loc.gov/2022042737
LC ebook record available at https://lccn.loc.gov/2022042738

∞™ The paper used in this publication meets the minimum
requirements of American National Standard for Information
Sciences—Permanence of Paper for Printed Library Materials, ANSI/
NISO Z39.48-1992

To every Young Man in the world,
the risk-takers and wanderers in pursuit of dreams

CONTENTS

ACKNOWLEDGMENTS

None of us escaped the gripping impacts of the pandemic unscathed, but we coped in different ways. In hard times, work was one stable place I could turn to for bits of sanity, stability, and even a glimpse of joy. This book is born out of those trying days.

Quite fortunately, the book was given expert treatment. Jennifer Lyons placed it, John Cerullo decided to publish it, Barbara Claire and Naomi Minkoff gave shape to it, and Jessica Kastner publicized it. Without their work, the book would be merely a floating vision. Chae Kyoung-sun, the unparalleled production designer of *Squid Game*, kindly granted me an interview despite her busy schedule. Thanks to her insights, this book was able to delve even deeper into the psychological maze of the games. Anupam Tripathi's reflections brought a kind presence to this book, just as his memorable character Ali Abdul (Player 199) was for the show. Patty Gone and Leslie Kriesel edited parts of the manuscript, bringing much-needed liveliness to what would have been a much stiffer narrative. Qianxiong Yang helped with research, allowing for the facile completion of the manuscript.

Just as *Squid Game* confronted us to face what really matters in life, the process of writing this book presented an equally urgent challenge for me. To say that "family and friends matter the most" is a cliché, but it is a cliché for a good reason. Satoko Shimazaki, Michael Emmerich, Ja-Hong Kim, Marc Levy, Andrea Goldman, Qiato Guo, Alex Wang, Hyeon-ju Rho, Moo Kyoung Lee, Eunhee Park, Josie Tong, Zachary Price, Leo Cabranes-Grant, Dan Jaffe, Todd Henry, and Lily and Francesco Bullo are local friends who make Los Angeles a more livable place. Julia Keblinska, Sookja Cho, Ana Hedberg Olenina, William Hedberg, Lucas Klein, Judit Kroo, Hyonjeong Kim, Jiayan Mi, Dao Mi, Chungmin Lee, Marco Milani, Antonio Fiori, Iljoong Kim, Amanda Stewart, Marlis Schweitzer, Sarah Bay-Cheng, Steven Lee, and Jinsoo An kindly provided various support for the project and invited me to their institutions to share the early iterations of this work. My gratitude also goes out to Eunjin Choi, Elaine Ho, Calvin

Wright, Miseong Woo, Hye Won Kim, Kyu Chan Cho, Yassi Jahanmir, Elena Zotova, and Lesya Kalynska. During the isolating times of the pandemic, I reconnected with my academic adviser and lifetime mentor, Professor Seog Young-joong of Korea University, whose formidable intelligence and spiritual depth resonate far beyond the walls of academia. It is because of her dedication to students that I find myself on this current path.

Living through many days and nights of the pandemic often felt like I was walking down a barely lit trail. When the candle blows out, someone has to stand up to light the pathway forward. In both good and bad times, my family kept standing there. Michael Berry is a person of many talents, not the least of which is coming up with best book titles. This book owes its name to my kindest soulmate. I am blessed with two high-spirited kids with a zest for exploration and adventure. Miles and Naima, every morning you bring greater brightness to fill the horizon of my life. My wise and caring mother-in-law Beverly St. John is always a model to emulate. My parents, siblings, and their children are branches of the same tree with shared roots that emanate vitality. At the end of my trail stands that tree.

Thanks to them, this book can gaze directly into the readers' eyes with full honesty.

INTRODUCTION

Local Arena for Global Games

Why *Squid Game?*

The world needed a fresh wheel to spin a story: to rise above the familiar tropes of Shakespearean intrigue, *Star Wars* battleships, and feel-good romances between surreally attractive celebrities. The pandemic-jaded world craved something new, something raw, something that would open our eyes to the new rules of making drama—a drama that would put us face-to-face with characters whose moral struggles would make us tremble and who would become our emphatic surrogates to confront the life-and-death matters that we do not want to be faced with in reality.

Upon its release on Netflix on September 17, 2021, *Squid Game* rattled the world, still held hostage to the pandemic lockdown. This genre-bending story about desperate contestants playing a series of deadly children's games for a multimillion-dollar cash prize became the first Asian-language drama to top Netflix's global chart. Not stopping there, its gory yet moving dramatic metaverse set social media platforms on fire, generating billions of TikTok memes and hundreds of parody games on Roblox within days of its initial release. Commenting on the gripping and galvanizing drama, Netflix co-CEO Ted Sarandos gave *Squid Game* odds for being more than a standout in foreign language titles, saying, "There is a very good chance it's going to be our biggest show ever." Indeed, less than a month from its release date, *Squid Game* easily surpassed *Bridgerton* and became the most watched drama in Netflix's history to date (see figure on the following page).

While *Squid Game* was still dominating global Netflix streaming, a highly anticipated film of the year, *Dune*, was released simultaneously on HBO Max and in multiplex theaters on October 21, 2021. With a pantheon of A-list stars and Denis Villeneuve behind the camera, the adaptation of Frank Herbert's famed *Dune* novel series dazzled viewers with its breathtaking scenery, immaculate CGI (computer-generated imagery) effects, sophisticated costumes, and sonorous sound design. But at the end of the

Korean promotional poster for *Squid Game* announcing
the release of the show on September 17, 2021.
ENTERTAINMENT PICTURES / ALAMY STOCK PHOTO

two-and-a-half-hour saga, there was hardly any emotional
ripple created by the characters in the film. Nor was there
any room for mere mortals to relate to this solemn parable
about a crisis of humanity set in the distant future. Like
the surface of a frozen lake, this megabudget film's wonder
lay in its outward beauty rather than the intricate yet real
psychological labyrinth connecting its characters.

At the same time as *Squid Game* was dominating the
pop culture conversation, the top three movies were super-
hero flix produced by either Disney or Sony Pictures.
Shang-Chi, *Venom*, and *Black Widow* astounded viewers

with flying bracelets in flames, a serpentine tongue dripping poisonous secretions, and synthetic bodysuits tight enough to suffocate the heroes even before they confronted the villains. But they didn't come close to capturing the deep despair of today's Everyman, struggling with financial pressures and gambling their lives to survive another day.

So why not *Squid Game*?

Never in Netflix's history had one drama series instantaneously become the topic of conversation around the entire globe. Even a few months after the show's release, new versions of *Squid Game*–inspired events and merchandise emerged, from Halloween costumes to Squid cryptocurrency (see figure on the following page).

What made *Squid Game* a runaway hit? Among countless factors, that it presented just the right balance between the familiar and unfamiliar elements might top the list. In the world of *Squid Game*, familiar events unfold on a strange planet. We all played red light, green light at some point in our childhood, but most of us had never heard of squid game before the show's eponymous title went viral. Most of us can relate to the crippling economic hardships created by COVID-19, but not many would have related it to a Korean pauper's habit of drinking *soju*, cheap Korean alcoholic beverage, with dry noodles sprinkled with instant

Squid Game Halloween costumes on display in a Southern California mall. PHOTO BY MICHAEL BERRY

soup powder. We might be very familiar with *The Hunger Games*, but we have not seen a death game thriller grafted onto a mundane family drama where a pathetic middle-aged man ends up doing something extraordinary against his will.

The local/global mélange of the show goes beyond the thematic hybridity. Broader forces are at work here—the encounter between the idiosyncrasies of Korean drama (K-drama hereafter) and the global streaming platform operating in more than 190 countries. *Squid Game* is a child born of a union between K-drama and Netflix, having inherited only the dominant genes from each parent. From the former it inherited a dense storytelling technique that values emotion over action. From the latter came the iconoclastic production model free of censorship restrictions. Without understanding this fruitful marriage, we cannot truly get to the bottom of *Squid Game*'s success. K-drama and Netflix found each other at a critical moment when the race for global media dominance was becoming increasingly tense.

So was this marriage a loving relationship that developed organically over time, or was it a calculated union between two experienced parties? In the whirlwind created by intensifying streaming wars, of course the latter is true, but there is also a slight hint of the former. Netflix gave K-dramas creative freedom and a higher production budget. K-drama, in turn, gave Netflix cost-effective hit shows guaranteed to increase the number of subscribers. Before partnering up with Netflix, K-drama was already a highly influential player with a notable following, its fame reaching far beyond Asia. Long before the Korean pop culture boom known as *hallyu* swept the Asia-Pacific region at the turn of the millennium, Korea had a thriving TV drama genre that became the true national pastime. Particularly strong in family drama, romantic melodrama, and historical costume drama, successful K-dramas provided a collective ritual for the nation whereby family members spent time together in the comfort of their home theaters. These dramas' social pervasiveness was such that people from different walks of life bonded over their favorite characters, while strangers might enter a heated debate over a drama's ending.

Squid Game's sweeping success prompted many to ask how Korean-language dramas were able to gain such a considerable following beyond their national borders. Lessons in history will help start this conversation. As a middle power, Korea has advantages in reaching out to a truly diverse global audience. Historically, Korea has not carried out imperialist expansion into other nations. Unlike Japan, it does not grapple with the ghosts of colonial conquest and military warfare that wreaked havoc in the transpacific world, still haunting many former colonies with deep trauma. Nor does Korea exercise geopolitical dominance like the United States, which invites vocal resistance from many nation-states, especially from the Global South. To be sure, pop culture is by no means subservient to the logic of realpolitik, but geopolitical confrontations could create cultural resistance, such as the Chinese government's current restrictions on Hollywood films. While Korea's middle-power status exempts the country from these conflicts, its rapid transformation into a sizeable economic powerhouse in the past five decades gave it the resources to develop an influential cultural industry. In other words, Korea was not a big enough political power to invite cultural resistance from others yet was economically big enough to cultivate a strong media and cultural industry. Present-day Korea boasts a vibrant media industry, with nine TV stations and a high concentration of talent pools. The drama industry is saturated with charismatic actors, clever storytellers, and hard-working production staff to meet the high expectations of demanding viewers. The director of *Squid Game* even noted that "Korean audiences tend to be more sensitive to trendiness, more unforgiving critics than those elsewhere. It is difficult to satisfy Korean audiences, whose support creators have worked tirelessly to win. Their high standards raised the bar for creators."[1] Like today's K-pop fans, K-drama viewers are unforgiving critics, which is the most significant factor that keeps elevating the quality of K-dramas to new heights.

THE GENESIS OF K-DRAMAS

Squid Game may have been the first experience with drama from Korea for the vast majority of global viewers, but its storytelling power emerges out of rich experience that spans nearly six decades. The history of Korean TV coincides with the advent of contemporary Korea as a hybrid society that underwent extremely rapid development. A nation that had very limited contact with the rest of the world until the late nineteenth century, Korea made a hyper-rapid transformation in the twentieth century, spanning political, economic, social, and cultural developments. These changes, which took place over several centuries in other places, were condensed into just a few decades in Korea. Korean sociologist Chang Kyung-sup [Jang Gyeong-seop] called this radical leap forward "compressed modernity"—a dizzying pace of change in the name of progress: "The sheer tempo and amount of unprecedented economic and social transformations so amazed people as to create a hypnotic state, in which various serious problems and costs accruing to such transformations did not immediately irritate their senses."[2] In this crash course in development, the dissonance between the rapid changes and the lagging perceptions about those changes warped the linear sense of time: tradition abandoned in pursuit of modern life kept haunting the new era, while the indigenous cycle of life kept interfering with a sense of progress. In this bewildering world, dramas were like mirrors held up to the face of a distorted nation, made to reflect its confusing dreams and aspirations as well as its darkest nightmares about those who fell behind along the way.

Nestled within the complexity of modern Korean history is the evolution of conventions of drama production in Korea. In the 1960s and '70s, television sets were starting to be distributed and the major broadcasting stations—KBS, MBC, and TBC—began to produce popular dramas catering mostly to female viewers. Due to women's extremely limited participation in the workforce, the TV drama audience during this time period was imagined to be primarily women. The 1970s and '80s saw even wider distribution of TV sets among middle-class households. This was also the time when multi-episode miniseries on an epic scale, including KBS's *6.25* (1977) and TBC's *Genealogy* (*Jokbo*, 1978), came into vogue because TV viewers were craving a new drama form that diverged from jaded stereotypes. The epic production scale of these miniseries was in large part influenced by ABC's *Roots* (1977), which aired in Korea to critical acclaim. Other popular American miniseries—*The Six Million Dollar Man* (1973–1978), *Little House on the Prairie* (1974–1983), *Dallas* (1978–1991), *The Incredible Hulk* (1978–1982), and *V* (1984–1985)—captured the imagination of Korean TV viewers with their astonishing array of subject matter and dynamic narrative structures spanning multiple seasons.

The 1990s marked a turning point for South Korean society. A much more relaxed social atmosphere emerged as a result of the transition from military dictatorship to civilian government, permission for foreign travel for civilians, and the lifting of the ban on Japanese culture. Along with these changes came a diversifying cultural appetite, curious to experience what lay beyond the domineering American culture. "Globalization" became a key word of the decade, and drama productions became much more diverse in their outlook. Historical dramas based on Joseon dynasty chronicles, such as the famed *Tears of the Dragon* (*Yong-ui nunmul*, 1997), invited male viewers to join in family TV time, presenting intriguing allegories to address the political predicaments of the era. Among countless iconic dramas of the 1990s, *Sandglass* (*Morae sigye*, 1995) came to occupy a special place in the history of K-drama. With its epic historical outlook that commemorated major events of South Korea's long twentieth century, *Sandglass* became a highly regarded documentation of Korean life. It was this drama that allowed Lee Jung-jae, Player 456–cum-winner of *Squid Game*, to debut to a phenomenal success and set him on the course to become one of South Korea's leading actors. (More on this in the next chapter.)

Long before K-pop dominated global arenas and Korean films topped international film festivals, K-dramas were at the forefront of the Korean culture boom. K-drama's global reach came at the turn of the millennium. Signaling the beginning of a Korean cultural vogue in China was lighthearted family drama *What Is Love* (*Sarang-i meogilae*, 1991–1992), which aired in mainland China in 1997 to enormous popularity. Following suit was seraphic romance melodrama *Winter Sonata* (*Gyeoul yeonga*, 2002). Creating a colossal sensation in Japan in 2003, it opened the way for other Korean dramas to enjoy the limelight there.

But a drama with true global reach was *Jewel in the Palace* (*Daejanggeum*, 2004), a fusion historical drama about a female palace attendant who rises to claim the top palace chef position by sheer talent and virtue alone. The drama's influence was felt in every corner of the world with a substantial Asian population. From new Korean restaurants named Jewel in the Palace in major global cities to increased demand for consumer goods, the market for products and services that carried the label "Made in Korea" increased. To lipstick manufacturers and the Korean Ministry of Culture, Sports, and Tourism alike, it became clear that highly successful dramas can have an enormous impact, boosting Korea's export-driven economy.

How to account for the exponential rise in K-drama's popularity? In addition to the external cultural thaw and ensuing freedom of expression, are there intrinsic characteristics that weave inimitable patterns in K-dramas? Given that the programs themselves are becoming increasingly diverse in genres and subjects, we cannot resort to broad generalizations, but one thing is certain: K-dramas present an effusive celebration of human conflicts and relationships. Even the attributes ascribed to action heroes that rely on interpersonal relationships matter more than awe-inspiring action skills (think *My Name*, a 2021 Netflix original). In other words, emotions fuel action, and entangled relationships are the true locomotives of storytelling. When Park Hae-soo [Bak Hae-su] and Jung Ho-yeon [Jeong Ho-yeon], Player 218 and Player 67 in *Squid Game*, were asked what made the show resonate so well with global audiences, they did not hesitate to respond: "human [drama]" and "story, the power of story," respectively.[3]

K-drama's consummate feast of emotional complexity has often given rise to hackneyed dramatic devices like memory loss, incest, taboo marriages between the rich and the poor, and revenge plots—*Autumn in My Heart* (*Gaeul donghwa*, 2000) and *Stairway to Heaven* (*Cheongugui gyedan*, 2003) being two prime examples. Other dramas, such as *Temptation of Wife* (*Anaeui yuhok*, 2008) and *Winter Bird* (*Gyeoulsae*, 2008), offered more sensational portrayals of extramarital affairs and bitter conflict between mothers-in-law and daughters-in-law as cheap gimmicks to attract a larger viewership. Often shot in intense close-ups, family conflicts bursting with highly charged emotions created the climax of many productions. Much to the dismay of domestic and international fans, these elements have often turned the K-drama world into an encyclopedia of clichés, but with repeated trial and error, they are gradually being sublimated into finely tuned human drama featuring relatable characters with intricate emotions.

Many of the troubled family relationships in K-dramas present a microcosm of broader social issues of injustice, the wealth gap, and class conflict. Executive producer Kim Iljoong [Gim Il-jung] of EastFormat—a subsidiary of Seoul Broadcasting Station created in 2019 to develop original programs for export—reflected upon the reason behind the success of K-dramas: "Korean programs excel in presenting grave social issues via easily understandable format. 'Global in concept, facile in content' is the key to successful format development."[4] Kim gives *Parasite* and *Squid Game* as prime examples where the global problem of the increasing wealth gap is presented through gaming formats (literal games in *Squid Game* and a series of cat-and-mouse games of deceit in *Parasite*). "Global in concept, facile in content" applies to the most influential K-dramas, which tackle the near impossibility of social mobility.

Another defining feature of K-drama is its use of cliff-hanger endings. Notorious for torturing viewers with tantalizing clues about what comes next, episode finales are addictive and invite binge watching. Unlike the vast majority of US dramas, in which each episode has some degree of autonomy and closure, K-drama endings feature suspense and thrill that come with open endings, luring the viewers to keep on watching episode after episode. Allow me to use a driving metaphor here: American dramas come back to a parking lot at the end of each episode, but Korean episodes end in a full-speed race on a superhighway. K-drama series made for domestic TV are released in installments on a weekly basis, so viewers have to wait a whole week to get a new episode. During that unbearable period of waiting, the internet fan community becomes a boiling pot brimming with discussions of the previous episode's high and low points and predictions for the show's ending. Some die-hard fans even write to TV stations with pleas to ensure a happy ending for their beloved characters. Unlike the typical weekly release model, Netflix enabled a onetime release of all nine episodes of *Squid Game*, eliminating the waiting. Nonetheless, thanks to the cliffhanger ending structure, this release adapted for binge watching did not sacrifice the intense feeling of suspense.

Just think of how episode 4 ends. Main characters we have come to know well—Gi-hun, Sang-woo, Ali, Il-nam, Sae-byeok, Ji-yeong, and even the manipulative Mi-nyeo—are on the verge of facing collective death. In an unfortunate tug-of-war game featured in the ominously

Gi-hun and Sang-woo face crisis in the "Tug of War" game, since their team will have to compete with a stronger opposing team. ENTERTAINMENT PICTURES / ALAMY STOCK PHOTO

titled episode "Stick to the Team," they are matched with an all-male team of stronger opponents (see figure above).

As our protagonists are pulled closer and closer to the edge of the disconnected bridge designed to make the losing team plunge to their death, nail-biting suspense heightens further. Precisely at this threshold moment, brainy Sang-woo proposes a risky gamble: take three steps forward to disturb the balance of their opponents. At this Borgesian fork, everyone takes three steps forward, then the screen blacks out. It's the end of the episode. Who can go to bed without finding out whether Sang-woo's gamble paid off, without knowing whether these beloved characters get to live another day?

Cliffhanger endings certainly make *Squid Game* an undeniable descendent of Korean entertainment media, but the closest genetic traits are found in the show's courtship of family melodrama. A time-honored tradition of Korean theater, TV, and film, tight-knit family life is at the forefront of most interwoven story lines. While the expression of family melodrama has often degenerated into stereotypes in the past, *Squid Game* replaced most of these weary devices with toned-down realism. When Gi-hun finds his mother dead and alone, the typical K-drama scene would have him wail, calling out for his dead mother in vain, flailing on the floor. Instead, *Squid Game* has him lie down quietly next to her, murmuring pointless words to convey his deep shock and exhaustion. Likewise, another potentially saccharine moment of family bonding—Sae-byeok's visit to her little brother in an orphanage—is restrained by her taciturnity.

The most melodramatic moment in *Squid Game* involves voluntary sacrifice. A newfound sisterhood between Sae-byeok and Ji-yeong has to end in Ji-yeong's voluntary death. Similarly, when Il-nam willingly gives Gi-hun his last remaining marble so that his *gganbu*, friends who share everything, can live, viewers' emotional gravity shifts from suspense to mourning. While many melodrama-jaded Korean fans criticized this moment for being inconsistent with the rest of the drama's unforgiving tone, foreign fans found this a refreshing moment of discovering new rules to weave a story. In *Squid Game*, no single nuclear family appears as the nodal point of storytelling, as in many other K-dramas, and yet what we have is a *Modern Family* Korean redux—a reflection of reality in twenty-first-century Korea, with its aging population, influx of migrant workers, and disintegration of the traditional family unit. *Squid Game* is a microcosm of the alternative kinship that emerges in the place of the dismantled traditional family unit. Undocumented people (Ali), social outcasts (all players, but Deok-su's retinue in particular), and North Korean defectors (Sae-byeok) all forge quasi-familial ties in a dormitory the size of an airplane hangar–cum–killing field (see figure on the following page). What emerges is a variation of K-melodrama updated in tune with the altered reality of present-day Korea.

A hybrid genre called *yeneung* has also had a formative influence, propelling the growing global reach of Korean TV programs. An amalgamation of everything and anything that entertains, *yeneung* is a genre-bending

In *Squid Game*, people from various walks of life forge a new type of kinship. ENTERTAINMENT PICTURES / ALAMY STOCK PHOTO

entertainment format that mixes elements of talk shows, quiz shows, cooking shows, elimination survival shows, audition shows, dramatic storytelling, and more. But the staple format of both shows has the hosts mingle with their guests in playing all sorts of games that demand physical prowess. A voracious monster devouring all things entertaining, *yeneung* programs such as *Running Man* (*Reoningmaen*, 2010–present) and *Infinite Challenge* (*Muhan dojeon*, 2005–2018) enjoyed phenomenal popularity across Asia, where they often became the highest-rated shows.

Squid Game comes off as a hybrid show blending dramatic storytelling and *yeneung* game formats. It embraces many elements of *Running Man* and *Infinite Challenge*: both feature five to seven hosts who are top celebrities in their own right, and every episode invites new guests who mingle with the hosts and compete in a variety of games, from ballroom dance competition to sporting events. The relationship between host and guests is analogous to that of *Squid Game*, in which game hosts Front Man and Oh Il-nam invite new contestants to play year after year. The fact that Front Man and Oh Il-nam participate in games themselves is also similar to *Running Man* and *Infinite Challenge*. *Infinite Challenge*, in particular, featured many episodes where the hosts played the same games featured in *Squid Game*—red light, green light, tug-of-war, and *ddakji*, or the flipping of folded paper disks—as if foreshadowing the rise of *Squid Game* as a fusion drama that mixes elements of *yeneung* with drama. For most global viewers of *Squid Game*, these Korean games might have come across as entirely novel, but viewers of Korean *yeneung* across the Asia-Pacific region were already familiar with games introduced through popular Korean entertainment shows. The dependence of *yenuengs* on competitive games and their enormous regional popularity made conditions ripe for *Squid Game* to resonate globally.

At the same time, *Squid Game* is an outlier of K-drama due to its campy yet realistic depiction of physical violence and psychological horror that would have been impossible to show prime-time TV audiences in Korea. In traditional dramas made for domestic terrestrial and cable TV stations, rambunctious creativity does not go unchecked by the Korea Communications Standards Commission (Bangsongtongsinsimui wiwonhoe), a regulatory board established in 1981 to filter out unsavory elements from the family-friendly environment of home theaters. Just take a look at South Korea's Broadcasting Act, article 6, "Impartiality and Public Interest Nature of Broadcasting," written by the commission:

6-3. A broadcast shall respect the ethical and emotional sentiments of the people, and contribute to safeguarding the fundamental rights of the people and the advancement of international friendship.

6-7. A broadcast shall extend its social education function, and diffuse and disseminate useful current information, and contribute to the qualitative improvement of the people's cultural life.

6-8. A broadcast shall contribute to the propagation of standard language, and endeavor to refine and purify the language.

Behind this regulatory practice lies a socially shared sentiment that dramas are common goods that belong to the public rather than private investors or companies. This broadly shared view in the K-drama world creates resistance against excessive profit-seeking activities that take place around drama productions—product placement being one example. Commercial breaks, for this reason, will not be favorablly received in Korea; breaking up an episode of a K-drama with commercials would cause a nationwide boycott against the product the following day.

The mandate of social edification in service of the public requires K-dramas to play it safe on the TV screen, compounded by the problems of limited budgets, harsh working conditions for the actors and production team, and impossibly short production timelines. The notorious *jjokdaebon*, or the practice of handing over a partial script written on the day of shooting, is a case in point. These challenging working conditions give K-drama production teams little choice but to follow the formula with a proven success record, leading to the jaded repetition of familiar story lines and also severely compromise the working conditions of nonunion workers, who become experts in improvising under duress.

Partnership with Netflix enabled the producers of *Squid Game* to bypass these rules. Count how many times the series broke the aforementioned "Impartiality and Public Interest Nature of Broadcasting" article. Director and screenwriter Hwang Dong-hyuk acknowledged that Netflix dramas "definitely have the advantage of enabling the creators freedom of expression on the matters that previously have been forbidden on commercial TV."[5] A dystopian take on the moral bankruptcy of the phenomenally rich and the predicaments of the economically disenfranchised, *Squid Game* was able to venture out to edgy terrain to express familiar themes of social injustice. This creative freedom was something the production team of *Squid Game* gained at the expese of forfeiting the profit-sharing model. It is true that the hardworking production team of *Squid Game* did not retain any intellectual property rights as a subcontractor to Netflix, creating a gaping unequal profit share. Paradoxical as it may be that a drama about socioeconomic inequality was produced and circulated by an unequal profit-sharing model, even a bigger irony looms large here: although many have criticized the extremely lopsided profit-sharing model between Siren Pictures (the Korean production company of *Squid Game*) and Netflix, it paradoxically presented a step up in the

eyes of the Korean production team. Being paid the production cost upfront meant the creators of *Squid Game*
could focus on the making of the drama with full artistic
autonomy, unburdened by the stress of either fundraising
or dealing with the consequences of the drama's potential
financial failure.

To better understand this irony, we must reflect upon
the brief history of how the drama production models and
financial structures have evolved in Korea throughout the
past three decades. Prior to the 1990s, TV drama production and distribution were led by the terrestrial TV stations such as MBC, KBS, and TBC, each having its own
pool of actors and a production team who signed exclusive
contracts with their TV stations. Much like the Hollywood studio system, these broadcasting companies (typically referred to as *jisangpa* in Korean) recruited their own
talents for self-produced shows to be aired on their own
channel. This model changed in the 1990s when the Korea
Communications Standards Commission imposed a quota
system on broadcasting stations to air dramas produced
by independent production companies (typically known
as *oejujejaksa* in Korean). This outsourcing production
policy—devised with the intention of (1) preventing the
monopoly of programming rights by large broadcasting

companies and (?) grooming a diverse range of production companies outside the terrestrial broadcasting system—was first introduced in 1990 and implemented in 1991.

The production outsourcing quota was a modest 3 percent in 1991, but it increased over time, reaching roughly 35 percent in 2022. For instance, according to the 2010 Announcement on Broadcast Programs (Bang-songpeurogeuraem deungui pyeonseonge gwanhan gosi 2010.2.3.) Protocol 8, broadcasting companies have the following quota requirements to air programming produced by independent production companies: in the case of Korean Broadcasting System KBS1, minimum 24 percent; KBS2, minimum 40 percent; multimedia broadcasting channel, minimum 20 percent.[6] According to the latest announcements by the Korea Communications Standards Commission (effective January 1, 2022), broadcasting companies and comprehensive programming (jongpyeon chaeneol in Korean), which stands for channels programming all genres, including news, documentaries, dramas, and variety shows, must air a minimum of 10 percent outside programming.

The relationship between the broadcasting companies and the independent drama production companies is changing according to the shifting media landscape, but it can best be described as hierarchical, with the former bearing 70 to 80 percent of production cost while the latter yields 100 percent of the intellectual property rights to the former. The remaining 20 to 30 percent of production costs had to be raised by the independent production company by means of product placement and other forms of fundraising.

The outsourcing production policy fueled a fierce rivalry among independent production companies, driving up production costs as they waged war to cast top stars, directors, and screenwriters to edge out the competition. (The exclusive contract system between broadcasting companies and talent came to an end in 1998, freeing talent to maximize their profit as freelancers.) Such inflated production cost is the reason behind the broadcasting system's partial support of the production cost (70 to 80 percent as opposed to 100 percent of the total production cost), bringing about many unwanted side effects, such as excessive product placements that disturbed the flow of storyline.

It was only in the 2000s that the independent companies started to demand more artistic autonomy and a bigger slice of the profit-sharing pie. They asked the broadcasting companies to share distribution rights and intellectual property rights. Broadcasting companies now provide roughly 50 percent of the production costs and share distribution rights with the independent production companies. Having a share in distribution rights means that independent production companies must work hard to sell their drama rights across Asia and beyond to generate extra profit. This may result in a huge success for independent production companies, as was the case with *Winter Sonata* (produced by Pan Entertainment and sold to NHK in 2003, igniting a huge cultural sensation in Japan and financial boon for Pan Entertainment). But these bright success stories are often outweighed by cases of failure, where the profit-sharing model may bring financial peril to the production companies. Sharing profits and distribution rights cannot happen without sharing risks.

Considering the history of K-drama production methods, the Netflix model of paying production costs upfront was attractive to Korean production companies, since it eliminated the headache of selling distribution rights and the worries about potential financial failure. Because of this safety net, *Squid Game* was able to flirt with sensational forms of expression and launch a genre-bending experiment, freely gliding over thriller, *yeneung*, family drama, cartoons, death games, and Asia extreme. K-drama was ready to enter orbit via the global streaming platform, hoping to unburden itself of the old constraints.

HERE COMES NETFLIX

Now let's turn to Netflix. Although its history is much shorter than the history of K-drama, Netflix went through equally drastic transformations. The company today is the undisputed leader of streaming platforms, but its beginning was characterized by uncertainties typical of many startups in the dot-com bubble era. Netflix took its first step as an outlier to Blockbuster, a media distribution and rental behemoth owned by the largest mass-media and entertainment conglomerate of the time, Viacom. Founded in 1997, Netflix bet on the future scenario that VHS would be phased out and replaced by DVDs, which, in turn, would give way to streaming services. The bet paid off handsomely. Netflix cofounder Reed Hastings recalls in a coauthored biography, *No Rules Rules*, that in 2002 the company value of Netflix was a meager $50 million (US) in comparison to the $5 billion of Blockbuster. By 2019, there was only one Blockbuster store remaining in the world, whereas Netflix had 167 million subscribers in 190 countries.[7] The only countries with no Netflix service in 2022 are China, North Korea, Russia, Syria, and Crimea—all either under US trade sanctions or engaged in a trade war.

Hastings looks back on the juncture where this dramatic reversal of fates took place as he identifies what Netflix had that Blockbuster did not: "a culture that valued people over process, emphasized innovation over proficiency, and had very few controls." But behind this congratulatory proclamation, Netflix also suffered self-inflicted harm along the way. When the company announced a 60 percent monthly fee raise in 2011, the company lost "600,000 subscribers, about 2 percent of its total customers at the time."[8] The same year, the company announced the separation of its DVD rental and video streaming services, to be represented by Qwikster and Netflix, respectively. These decisions caused Netflix's value to plummet; the company scrapped Qwikster just a month after announcing the launch plan, and Hastings offered repeated public apologies.

Meanwhile, a streaming war intensified, with competitors such as HBO Max, Amazon Prime, and Disney+ vying for the attention of over-the-top (OTT) consumers who stream content over the internet to satisfy their individual needs and tastes. A pivotal moment for Netflix came in 2016 when, in a move to differentiate itself from these competitors, the company announced its global strategy to expand its service to 130 countries. Announcing the move in a keynote speech at the Consumer Electronics Show, Hastings promoted the idea of customer freedom based on the ability to choose their viewing time: "I am delighted to announce that while we have been here on stage at CES we switched Netflix on in Azerbaijan, in Vietnam, in India, in Nigeria, in Poland, in Russia, in Saudi Arabia, in Singapore, in South Korea, in Turkey, in Indonesia, and in 130 new countries. . . . Today, right now, you are witnessing the birth of a global TV network."[9] Global expansion meant that Netflix was adopting a more diversified distribution model as well as increased modes of multilingual production. From "the world's largest online DVD rental service" (2002) to "the world's largest online movie rental service" (2009)—and then from "the world's leading Internet subscription service for enjoying TV shows and movies" (2011) to "global internet TV network" (2017)—Netflix's self-proclaimed identity has evolved along with its global outlook and changing distribution technologies.[10]

Netflix's adaptability in circulating its media content prompted media scholar Timothy Havens to label it a "tech company more than a media company." For Havens, Netflix builds its brand identity around distribution: "Netflix

. . . draws a number of associations related to its *service*, rather than its programming, to brand itself as disruptive, youthful, individualistic, techy, and capable of satisfying immediate viewer desire. All these elements operate at the level of the corporate brand, emphasizing the experience of streaming television over any particular content."[11] But even though Havens places much emphasis on the technical side of the company, Netflix is equally concerned with content and distribution. Its aspirational billboard sign on Sunset Boulevard confirms this point loud and clear: "Don't Give Up on Your Dreams. We started with DVDs." This mantra underlines its ambition to create new streaming content as much as its desire to innovate forms of distribution.

If Netflix's early transition from DVDs to online streaming revolutionized media distribution, its transition from renting out DVDs made by other companies to producing its own original series was equally groundbreaking. The first series to create a notable sensation were *House of Cards* (2013–2018) and *Orange Is the New Black* (2013–2019), signaling the era of the Netflix originals. The subscription base increased due to the popularity of these shows, which were quickly followed by the equally memorable sagas *Narcos* (2015–2017) and *The Crown* (2016–present). While Netflix is known for series ranging from matters of British royal succession to the gritty underworld of drug trafficking, the platform also directed its resources to producing original bona fide cinema, much to the dismay of Hollywood studios. A case in point, during the premiere of *Okja*, directed by Oscar winner Bong Joon-ho, the audience booed when the Netflix logo appeared onscreen at the Cannes Film Festival, expressing loud and clear vociferous criticism at a non-studio-produced film being screened at one of the world's most prestigious film festivals. In a country like France, where cinema still occupies a privileged space in the cultural hierarchy, film scholars such as Ana Vinuela openly shared the critical sentiment about Netflix: "Would Netflix have produced *Squid Game* without *Parasite*?"[12] Likewise, Daniela Elstner, the executive director of UniFrance Film International, noted that "film has a symbolic place in France and Netflix is hoping to get part of it."[13]

In countering the prejudice against Netflix original films as ersatz versions of Hollywood studio cinema, the company strove to win legitimacy by partnering up with big-name directors. The likes of Shonda Rhimes, the Coen brothers, and Martin Scorsese directed films for Netflix, and it did not take long for the streaming giant to emerge with productions that garnered critical acclaim. Netflix-backed *Roma* was nominated for best picture at the 2019 Academy Awards and won three Oscars in the cinematography, directing, and international film categories. The year 2019 also saw the release of another highly acclaimed historical drama, *The King.* Unlike with *Okja,* just two years earlier, the audience at the Venice Film Festival premiere did not jeer, nor did the audience at BFI London Film Festival frown upon the film's alliance with Netflix distribution.

Netflix's efforts to authenticate itself continue. As part of its globalization process and part of its self-branding as a valid film production company, Netflix forged a partnership with La CinéFabrique, a film school in France, to "support school scholarships as part of the 'Education à l'image' program designed for young people with deep academic challenges. Those selected are given financing to produce their short films, access to Netflix executives and talent, as well as special writing classes covering serialized storytelling, and the chance to receive on-the-job training on Netflix productions like the upcoming season of *Lupin.*"[14] Furthermore, in September 2021 Netflix opened a massive brick-and-mortar production studio in Brooklyn. With six soundstages and flexible support space, the company is becoming increasingly similar to traditional film studios such as Paramount, Disney, and Universal Pictures.

Although Hastings in 2019 claimed that the company would focus more on pushing "the edge in entertainment" rather than entering the competition for a $500 million film production, Netflix is certainly blurring many boundaries between classic film studios and multiseries drama production companies catering to streaming platforms.

The unavailability of the movie theater experience during the early stay-at-home phase of COVID-19 accelerated the fusion between films made for theatrical distribution and TV dramas. Just think of how big-screen films such as Disney's *Mulan* and Marvel Studios' *Black Widow* had no choice but to premiere on OTT due to the prolonged lockdown. Temporarily liberated from competition with multiplex blockbuster films and other forms of in-person entertainment (concerts, nightclubs, and sporting events), Netflix seized the opportunity to play up its merit as a flexible platform where reputable film directors could flex their artistic muscles for viewers placed under involuntary house arrest. The fusion of what has been traditionally regarded as "highbrow" cinema and "lowbrow" TV shows can generate creative synergy in production–*Squid Game* being a prime example.

Hwang Dong-hyuk had never directed TV dramas, so the nine-episode megahit was his debut. His extensive career as a film director and screenwriter brought density to the storytelling (to be addressed more in the next chapter). In a conversation with director Bong Joon-ho, Hwang confessed that the longer running time of serial TV dramas allowed him to experiment with formats and introduce more dense characterizations not possible in the compact form of cinema.[15] Other OTT sites experienced a similar fusion of genres: popular Korean film director Kim Ji-woon, well known for eclectic blending of gore and art house cinema styles, directed *Dr. Brain* for Apple TV. Kim claimed that in dramas "cinematic mood or aura might lack relatively, but the storytelling function has become clear and laconic. I might go back and forth between drama and cinema for a while."[16] As Kim noted, such fusion appears to be an irreversible trend that will bring a cinematic-scale to dramas made for TV screens.

Netflix's success during the pandemic is in large part because its globalization strategy was well into its fourth year when the worldwide shutdown took place. Unlike film studios, which depend on active film shoots and new film releases, Netflix already had a huge depository of programs hailing from many parts of the globe. With physical theaters shut down, moviegoers had no choice but to explore yet-to-be-seen films and drama series already available on the streaming site. American viewers with increased time at their disposal rummaged through various Netflix international language categories they might not have noticed prepandemic.

Susan Kresnicka, business anthropologist and founder/president of KR&I, noted that American audiences, especially younger audiences, have come to watch an increasing number of global programs at home as a result of multilingual households: "Sixty percent of Gen Z and younger Americans watch non-English content at home. This consists of a mix of streaming and nonstreaming services. They grew up on the internet."[17] This easy access to and adoption of the internet as their natural habitat certainly made the conditions ripe for non-English language shows to be accepted at home without much resistance. But was the opposite also true, where international viewers investigated more American shows as well as other foreign shows produced outside the United States?

There are no available data to answer this question, but any effort to find answers must consider the entanglement of the local national media infrastructure and the incursion of the American streaming giant, which media scholar Ramon Lobato characterized as follows: "As a company that has internationalized very quickly, Netflix's story also tells us a lot about what happens when a digital service enters national markets, coming in over the top of existing institutions and regulations. Netflix, in other words, is a case study with larger relevance to ongoing debates in media studies about convergence, disruption, globalization, and cultural imperialism."[18] In response to such critical sentiment, here is what Hastings had to say in 2019: "If you produce a wide variety, you get lots of sharing around the world. Fundamentally we want to produce everywhere in the world."[19] No doubt a media tech giant like Netflix is always prone to spreading American dominance, and the initial stage of its globalization did export more US-produced content to global audiences.

But let's not forget to look at the flip side. Netflix's globalization strategy could be a movement to counter the lopsided flow of pop culture from the United States to the rest of the world. For instance, Christophe Riandee, vice CEO of Gaumont Television France, declared that "working with streamers is positive because it creates work for all."[20] Whether that is motivated by business calculations or by genuine concern for multilateral cultural respect is another story (more on that soon), Netflix's business model gave the company little choice but to cast its production net internationally.

Remember one clear principle: Netflix will follow wherever the profit is. Netflix's global outlook has much to do with how it used to generate profit solely based on a subscription model rather than advertising revenue. As of June 2022, there are neither commercial breaks nor product placements in Netflix content. That's all about to change due to the dramatic decline in subscribers and profit as the world gradually emerges from the pandemic.[21] But for the vast majority of Netflix's existence, expanding the number of subscribers was crucial to maintaining the ad-free streaming model. Today's Netflix subscribers are, for the most part, located in North America and Europe, with large untapped potential in Asia and Africa. The company's globalization strategy is part and parcel of expanding its subscription base worldwide.

Global production means global sharing, no doubt, but what 190 countries share currently is mostly made by a handful of countries concentrated in the Global North. In working through the issues of cultural influence, we should also take into consideration that "content imperialism" and "platform imperialism" are different, as noted by media scholar Hye-Jin Lee.[22] Netflix, as a giant platform with the vast majority of its streamed content originating in the United States, can be critiqued as propelling both content (made in Hollywood) and platform (Netflix, Disney, HBO, Amazon) imperialism; at the same time, the growing cultural influence of foreign content has the potential to foster small-scale content imperialism.

Production companies outside the United States mostly hail from the UK, France, Germany, and Spain. Prior to *Squid Game*, iconic miniseries from these countries paved the way for foreign shows to claim global popularity. *The Crown* might not be a straightforward example of this, since it is a coproduction between Left Bank Pictures in the UK and Sony Pictures Television in the United States, but it nevertheless introduced much British acting talent to global audiences. Other European shows, such as Spain-produced *Money Heist* (*La Casa de Papel*, 2017–2021), Germany-produced *Dark* (2019), and France-produced *Lupin* (2021), whetted global viewers' appetite for crime-thrillers with a foreign bent to command enormous popularity, paving the way for *Squid Game*'s emergence.

Money Heist, in particular, shares many similarities with *Squid Game*. Although the two are quite different in narrative cadence, directorial tone, and method of character depiction, they overlap in key design elements. It was *Money Heist* that first garbed boundless greed and violence in pink suits and absurd masks (see figure on the following page).

The Spanish-language drama *Money Heist* introduced to Netflix a crime thriller with pink suits and strange masks. BY DRONEPICR–

The show's heightened popularity extended its run to five seasons and prompted Netflix to produce the Korean remake in twelve episodes.[23] *Dark*, on the other hand, introduced a much more psychologized version of the thriller genre—an intricate approach that *Squid Game* also takes. The dark ambience of the show allowed for deeper portrayal of the characters' interior space, which at times bordered on horror and nightmares. Although the visual designs of *Dark* and *Squid Game* clearly differ, with the latter having much more playful kitsch and camp elements, they both use distinctive color palettes to paint the internalized terror of the bizarre rules of the world.

Not to be left out in the list of key global content providers is Japan. With its traditional strength in anime, horror, and Asia extreme, Japanese content attracts viewers who seek new genres and refreshing storytelling techniques. Japanese anime films in particular—from the classical *End of Evangelion* (1997) to newer productions such as *Children of the Sea* (2020), as well as highly intriguing series such as *Alice in Borderland* (2020–present)—fit Netflix's bill, providing "stories that people feel are unusual" or "something they haven't seen before."[24]

HAPPILY MARRIED AFTER?

The successful precedents of the aforementioned international shows include Korean TV dramas as well. Netflix had much reason to back the production of Korean originals. Korea's brand power as a cultural hub of trendiness is an influence that has long spilled out of Asia. K-dramas such as *Jewel in the Palace* have a proven track record of success across Asia, Africa, and the Arab world—places where Netflix has yet to expand its subscription base. Therefore, the seeds for a deep collaborative relationship had been sown before *Squid Game*. K-drama entered the world of Netflix with its first original series, *Love Alarm* (*Joahamyeon ullineun*, 2019, 2021), a fantasy romance based on the webtoon about an app that alerts users if someone with a romantic interest is in the vicinity. With their unique strength in crafting intense feelings and intricate human relationships, more Netflix originals from Korea entered the OTT universe.

The first to garner notable early success on Netflix was *Kingdom* (*Kingdeom*, 2019–2020), a fusion drama that crosses the genre boundaries of period drama, political thriller, and zombie horror. *Kingdom* was favorably received by film critics and fans alike, to the point that it inspired the French Netflix original *La Revolution* (2020), which deployed a similar concept of plague besetting eighteenth-century France on the eve of the French Revolution. Named one of the best international shows of 2020 by the *New York Times*,[25] *Kingdom* even saw its popularity spread to *gat*, the traditional Korean male hat, which became much sought-after online merchandise by global fans of the show. *Kingdom* thus helped seal the image of traditional Korea, so much so that the newly appointed Korean ambassador to Britain, Kim Gunn, wore *gat* and traditional Korean male attire when he submitted a letter of credence to Queen Elizabeth II on October 27, 2021.

Following the global success of *Kingdom* were romance dramas *It's OK Not to Be OK* (*Ssaikojiman gwaenchana*, 2020) and *Crash Landing on You* (*Sarangui bulsichak*, 2020). Unlike *Kingdom*, which ominously foreshadowed the global pandemic, *It's OK Not to Be OK* presented an unusual love story between a man who refuses to love and a woman who is incapable of love. Likewise, *Crash Landing on You* focused on the forbidden relationship between a North Korean man and a South Korean woman, but instead of resorting to the jaded framework of hostility between the two Koreas, the show cast the relationship in a refreshingly contemporary light. *Crash Landing on You* did particularly well in Japan, and many predicted a new Korean cultural boom in the country. *It's OK Not to Be OK* also did phenomenally well in many Asian countries, including Hong Kong, Thailand, Vietnam, Malaysia, and Japan, while also entering the Top 10 Netflix chart across South America. This notable success was soon followed by *Sweet Home* (*Seuwiteuhom*, 2020), the first K-drama to have entered the Top 10 US chart while ranking sixth on the global chart. Based on the popular webtoon series, *Sweet Home* fit the horror thriller genre popular on Netflix. As if riding on the momentum of *Kingdom*, it centered on the anxiety surrounding the slippery borderline between the human and the monstrous—a theme picked up once again by *All of Us Are Dead* (*Jigeum uri hakgyoneun*, 2022) to continue the genealogy of K-horror on Netflix.

Not only dramas but also *yeneung* programs have made their way into the Netflix universe. Netflix has been acquiring nonfiction Korean content on its site since the spring of 2017. Unlike the dominance of dramas, which claim their own category of K-drama, *yeneung* is placed under International Reality, Talk & Variety Shows alongside the likes of *Bollywood Wives*, *Dating around Brazil*, and *The Parisian Agency: Exclusive Properties*. While *yeneung* has a long way to go to claim as prominent a space on Netflix as K-dramas have, its presence is increasing, with more titles being added each year. Korea has a strong infrastructure for unique internet-based genres with potential to make successful *yeneung* shows. From video streaming service platforms based on peer-to-peer technology such as Afreeca TV to countless podcasts, the "guerilla-casting" model mushroomed and gave birth to unique Korean genres.[26] One is *meokbang*, which combines food porn and ASMR (an acronym for "autonomous sensory meridian response," referring to a tingling sensation people feel when watching a stimulating video) with culinary anthropology, speaking to an exponentially growing number of single-person households across the globe. *Meokbang* has become a global phenomenon, so much so that the word even entered the latest edition of the *Oxford English Dictionary*. Such rapid growth of the guerilla-casting model out of Korea can easily be subsumed by Netflix, a voracious platform with less discerning and less discriminative content regulations than traditional platforms.

These cases of cross-pollination between Netflix and Korean programs have nourished the ground for the kinds of smash success that *Squid Game* has come to enjoy. At the 2016 Consumer Technology Association Annual Meeting,

Hastings referred to Seoul as just another global city starting with "S": "Whether you are in Sydney or St. Petersburg, Singapore or Seoul, Santiago or Saskatoon, you now can be part of the internet TV revolution."[27] Today Seoul occupies a special place in the Netflix universe as a prolific provider of unique and edgy content that is also extremely cost-effective. But let's not forget that someone's gain is someone else's pain. Korean content's cost-effectiveness is a boon for Netflix, but what does it say about the level of compensation and work condition for supporting actors, extras, staff, designers, and writers?

Some comparisons can help us contextualize the situation. The production cost for one episode of *Squid Game* is $1.8 million (US). *Bridgerton*, which was the most viewed Netflix show prior to *Squid Game*, costs $7 million per episode. The production cost for one episode of *The Crown*, Netflix's most expensive drama to date, is a staggering $13 million.[28] For a small fraction of the production cost for its most iconic-yet-costly dramas, Netflix was able to create an astronomically larger impact with *Squid Game*. In an interview with the *Guardian*, director Hwang Dong-hyuk claimed he did not receive any bonus for the phenomenal success of his creation, since, as is the usual case with Netflix's global shows, content creators sign a "no-frills" contract up front and are not paid extra for streaming counts. Due to this model, content creators are not equal partners when it comes to sharing the fruits of their labor.

The euphoria emanating from *Squid Game*'s success in Korea was soon followed by a sobering reckoning of this lopsided profit-sharing model. The Korean drama world has long been dealing with the perpetual problems of an over-worked and underpaid labor force that is not unionized to protect working conditions. Behind the glitzy success lies painful human sacrifice, as we have seen in the multiple deaths of staff members for *Kingdom*. The long-standing ailment of the Korean entertainment industry—mani-fested in the pay gap between a handful of well-compen-sated lead actors and the large majority of underpaid extras and staff—is a highly sensitive topic that is now useful as a frame to understand the uneven relationship between the high production costs of European series and the low production costs of K-dramas on Netflix. Although part-nership with Netflix has brought about key improvements in the areas of creative freedom and increased production investment, it has created anxiety among Koreans worried about the "subordination of culture" and Korea's position as a fungible subcontractor to the global media force.[29] The sense of anxiety is shared by those who partner with

Netflix, such as Isabelle Degeorges, the producer of the French Netflix show *Lupin*, who confessed, "We don't know whether Netflix is a 'savior' or 'predator.'"[30]

Korea's troubled view on Netflix extended beyond the realm of content production. Netflix's subscription base in Korea has grown exponentially, having reached 5.14 million in 2021, compared with 3.16 million in 2020. OTT platform users in Korea spend more time on Netflix than on other platforms. With the increased use of bandwidth related to the increasing demand for Netflix, local internet providers' costs have gone up. SK Broadband, the South Korean provider of internet service for Netflix, claims that Netflix should provide financial compensation for the increased volume of internet traffic, as SK incurs massive expenses. In response, the South Korean government is closely considering new legislation to enable South Korean companies like SK to collect extra charges, while Netflix has been attempting to legally clarify the legitimacy of the extra network service bill.[31]

As a part of an attempt to assuage the situation, Netflix dispatched Singapore-based Vice President of Public Policy Dean Garfield to Korea in early November 2021. In a series of high-profile media events, Garfield delivered conventional lip service to Korean content creators, touting their exceptional success: "We are in the midst of a story-telling renaissance, with Korea leading the way. Korea is fast becoming one of the greatest and most influential entertainment and cultural centers in the world, not just K-drama, but also music, fashion [and food]. . . . The K-wave has infiltrated not just Asia, but every corner of the world. For example, *Squid Game* made it to number one on Netflix in 94 countries when it launched. We are so very excited to be a part of this journey with Korea."[32] Garfield's speech is a faithful reflection of Netflix's company mandates: to "act in Netflix's best interest" and that "a global company needs a global culture." Indeed, Netflix has entered the irreversible course of globalization, in which Korea has now become a partner they cannot afford to lose. But the merciless pursuit of business interests and the liberal spirit of global culture seldom see eye to eye.

According to Reed Hastings, "It's been so exciting for Netflix over the last few years to expand around the world. Now we understand much better how different nations like to give feedback, and it's been very stimulating for everyone at Netflix to be included, and all of these different values so that we can work well together to serve our members around the world."[33] Hastings shared his egalitarian spirit to characterize the company's global strategy, but when it comes to real issues, such as carrying the cost of broadband service or paying more competitive wages to Korean production teams, will it value the Korean perspective?

The mounting criticism of Netflix prompted the company to pay an undisclosed amount as a one-time bonus to the *Squid Game* team, but this was just a bandage placed on the open wounds of underemployment and inequitable partnership.[34] Netflix's prolonged marriage with Korea will inevitably generate thornier questions, such as fair profit distribution and sharing the cost of infrastructure, in the days to come. In order to play a global game, Netflix needs thriving local arenas like Korea. Likewise, for locally produced K-drama to have a worldwide reach, it needs a global window like Netflix. Time will tell how this marriage sustains itself, but a golden child like *Squid Game* will certainly help the rocky relationship meet happier days.

1

LET THE GAMES BEGIN

Strung tightly like roller-coaster trains, the nine episodes of *Squid Game* beckon us for a wild ride. Once the trains depart the station, a dizzying diorama captivates your eyes and ears with feigned merriment. As the gyrations come to a halt, vertiginous riders leave the station holding their churning stomach. They are terrified as much as intoxicated by the revolting quiver. The tense emotional thrill of *Squid Game* would not have been produced without the consummate artistry and exhaustive labor of the people working in the Korean film and drama industry. From novice production staffs to drivers who transported truckloads of cameras, each and every one of them deserves a standing ovation. This chapter will focus on the career paths of many of the seminal players who breathed *Squid Game* into being. Artistic director Chae Kyoung-sun, music director Jung Jae-il, and the key actors who are now globally recognized figures all enthused about this riveting drama, but we'll begin with the person who played this game harder and longer than anyone: Hwang Dong-hyuk.

THE DIRECTOR

Hwang Dong-hyuk claims he lost six teeth from stress while making *Squid Game*. Yet through that stress, the director and screenwriter somehow fused the creativity of all his collaborators into a dramatic island prison world of haunting music, cartoonish architecture, and grotesquely beautiful sets, all with base human longing and the will to survive at its core. According to *Squid Game*'s lead actor, Lee Jung-jae:

> Hwang is someone who always tries out new genres and tells different stories. *Squid Game* seems to be a culmination of everything he has previously produced. *Squid Game* features the intricate interpersonal feelings shown in *My Father*, an edgy and frightening story as in *Silenced*, jolly and humorous moments as in *Miss Granny*, and a profound theme as in *The*

Fortress. It felt like he wanted to show off all his skills in *Squid Game*.[1]

True to Lee's appraisal, Hwang's film career is marked by versatility. From family melodrama to crime comedy to somber war saga to a petrifying social problem film, Hwang transcends genre. Like director Ang Lee, who has helmed everything from Taiwanese family dramas to *Hulk*, Hwang's interests contain multitudes of subjects. Although his film career has not been as celebrated as fellow South Korean auteur directors Bong Joon-ho, Park Chan-wook, and Kim Ji-woon, just to name a few, Hwang's multiplicity of styles synthesizes in *Squid Game*.

Hwang's directorial debut came with *My Father* (2007), for which he wrote the script as well—a long-lasting professional habit that extended to the making of *Squid Game*. Based on the real-life story of Korean adoptee Aaron Bates, the film follows Bates on his search for his biological father, who ends up being a convicted murderer serving a life sentence. *My Father* works with one of the most enduring features of Korean narrative—the honorable quest for reconciliation of divided families. Although the film illustrated Hwang's craftmanship as a storyteller, it disappointed at the box office. In a 2017 interview, Hwang said,

"There was pressure to make an impressive debut. There were many aspects I could not do as I wished."[2] The film's failure put Hwang in a precarious situation, forcing him to move back in with his mother, just like the Player 456—an experience Hwang undoubtedly drew from for the script of *Squid Game*.

Hwang followed his first film with another docudrama based on another real-life event, *Silenced* (*Dogani*, 2011). But in contrast to the heartwarming tone of *My Father*, here he chose a disturbing incident that had rattled South Korean society a few years earlier: the sexual abuse of deaf and mute minors at Gwangju Inhwa School, a school for students with special needs. Like his previous work, Hwang wrote the script himself, and his direction creates a probing exposé of how powerless children, who literally cannot speak up for themselves, fall prey to physical and sexual abuse by a staff entrusted with educating and protecting them. In selecting their prey, the principal and fellow teachers at the school intentionally target students without capable legal guardians. Not just the school but other institutions, from the police to the church to the judiciary system, all impaired by corruption, fail to bring justice to the victimized minors. "My main goal was to reawaken people's attention to the incident,"[3] Hwang shared in an interview, recalling how his film, which opened to critical acclaim, was able to bring about actual social change. Partially due to the incendiary outcry the film created in the public, the so-called Dogani Law came into effect in South Korea on November 17, 2011, decreeing that anyone accused of sexually abusing disabled minors under the age of thirteen may be sentenced to life in prison.

The director's interest in the rights of the disenfranchised sheds light on the genesis of *Squid Game*. Although the Netflix megahit exhibits a much more nuanced portrayal of the powerless, who are at the same time also conniving, violent, and cruel, it was in *Silenced* that Hwang cultivated his vision of cinema's responsibility to expose social ailments as viscerally as possible. Philosopher Slavoj Žižek critiqued *Squid Game* as being a compliant endorser of capitalism while parading as anticapitalist. While this clever diagnosis may present an intriguing reading of the show (Netflix is a capitalist platform, and the show has certainly given the company a high return on their investment), obviously Žižek is unaware of *Squid Game*'s ideological roots, which harken back to *Silenced*—Hwang's cinematic turning point that laid the ground for the director to fully confront how capitalist commodification and transaction of life eat away at humanity. *Squid Game* arrived in front of so many eyes due to the capitalist enterprise Netflix, but it's still a morality play on a massive scale seen by a huge swath of the globe.

Silenced also forged a working relationship between Hwang and some of the actors who would appear in *Squid Game* a decade later. Kim Joo-ryung (Player 212) appears both calculating yet vulnerable in *Squid Game*, yet in *Silenced* she is a less complex villain who, without any remorse, participates in covering up her colleagues' sexual abuse; Lee Sang-hee (Player 017, aka the glass master), makes a brief appearance as a car mechanic in *Silenced*; Park Hye-jin (Sang-woo's mom), a warm and caring motherly figure in *Squid Game*, plays the terror-inspiring wife of the school principal who denies the horrific abuse of minors in *Silenced*. But the most notable reversal of roles comes with Gong Yu, the enigmatic man in *Squid Game* who invites Player 456 to the games at the metro station; in *Silenced,* Gong Yu is the dignified leading man, a young teacher who carries out a lonely fight against the corrupt society.

This thread between *Silenced* and *Squid Game* extends to the thematic level: in addition to exposing the gross failure of the society to protect its minors, both films lay bare the harrowing effects of a surveillance society. In *Silenced,* the principal of the school perversely captures sexual abuse on hidden cameras; in *Squid Game*, the counterpart is extensive use of surveillance, monitoring every movement of the players and the guards. Both films feature male protagonists' troubled relationships with their elderly mothers while themselves being absent father figures in their young daughters' lives. But the most compelling parallel between *Silenced* and *Squid Game* rests within the schizophrenic doubling of consciousness embodied in the figure of twins—a central motif that runs through Hwang's films. The chief abusers of disabled minors in *Silenced* are identical twin brothers, one of whom raped children while the other turned a blind eye; their indistinguishable looks confuse young victims when they are asked to identify the offender during the trial. In Hwang's later works, the casting of literal twins sublimates into figurative twins with opposite traits who in essence are split sides of the same entity. As will be seen in chapter 3, figurative twins become a hallmark device for Hwang, a way to stage the intricate moral dilemmas inside all of us.

In 2014, Hwang directed *Miss Granny* (*Susanghan geunyeo*), the first commercially successful film in his career. According to the director, he wanted to make a movie that "people in their 70s and 80s, who have never been to movies before, can easily enjoy with their grand-children."[4] Far from the revolting exposé of *Silenced*, this family comedy centers on a grandma, Oh Mal-sun, who often irks and annoys her family with her garrulous and overpowering personality. Although Mal-sun is a tough lady who has survived widowhood and single parenthood despite enormous hardship, she has a tender heart. The film gains narrative momentum when Mal-sun magically transforms into an adorable yet vagarious young woman who retains the personality traits of a grandma. Her uncanny rejuvenation wreaks havoc in the lives of her son's family, who ultimately come to understand and love her when she returns to her senior self. Distributed by CJ ENM, the film attracted 8.6 million viewers in Korea and was remade in China, Japan, Thailand, Vietnam, and Indonesia, to further commercial success.

Though it may seem to be a harmless family comedy, the film grapples with the conundrums of an aging society, a concern that resurfaces in *Squid Game*. *Miss Granny*'s opening scene takes place in a university seminar room where students discuss their bias against senior citizens. The professor leading the discussion is Mal-sun's son, a gerontologist caught between his bossy mother and his disgruntled wife, whose mutual strife creates a minor war zone in his home. Casting a senior citizen as the protagonist in *Miss Granny* finds a parallel in *Squid Game* with Oh Il-nam, Player 001, as the central catalyst with a stunning character reversal. Both present the elderly as true masterminds who shape the course of young people's lives. Hwang offers no easy solutions to the problem of the elderly being less powerful physically yet having more ability to manipulate systems where their concerns are no longer central.

Both works feature animated music boxes to create an ambivalent mood that obfuscates the boundaries between fantasy and reality, along with the horror and laughter that emerge from the co-presence of a grandmother and a young woman in the same body (more on this in chapter 3). Both also toy with the cliffhanger, a trope typical of K-drama: *Miss Granny* features an avid K-drama fan tortured with a tantalizing ending, while Hwang invoked the conventional dramatic device in every episode of *Squid Game*, with even the last one concluding on a note of nail-biting suspense. In one way, Hwang has given in to the convention, but he performs the convention so well that he must count K-drama as an influence. And finally, the jolly ambience of *Miss Granny* resonates with the cartoonish grandeur of *Squid Game*, which stylizes violence and gore into juicy spectatorial entertainment.

Anyone who has seen *The Fortress* (*Namhansanseong*, 2017) may doubt that it is directed by the same person who, just three years earlier, directed a harmless comedy about a shapeshifting grandma. Yet Hwang adapted Kim Hun's 2007 novel *The Fortress* into a somber war period piece based on one of the darkest moments of the Joseon dynasty. The action follows the Qing invasion of Joseon in 1636 when the newly installed emperor Hong Taiji advanced his army to Joseon. As King Injo and his Ming royalist government refuse to recognize Qing as the new emperor, they take refuge in the Namhan Mountain Fortress, forcing Joseon's impoverished and outsized army to carry out a futile forty-seven-day standoff with the formidable adversary. Hwang spatializes the king's feelings of isolation with the desolate fortress steeped in winter frost—captured by a straightforward camera move free of technical flair and stylistic embellishment.

The fortress's solemnity may at first strike us as an unlikely ancestor of the violent playground island of *Squid Game*. But if we consider the influences Hwang sketches out in the following interview, the lineage might not feel far-fetched: "I'd recently watched *Sicario*, *The Revenant*, and *Lost in Dust*. All three movies take place in desolate settings, but within those worlds lied the tight entanglement of the time, space, and people caught in friction. These were the ideal films that I always wanted to shoot."[5] Characters living inside a tinderbox cut across the spatial settings of both *The Fortress* and *Squid Game*: both productions mix agonized faces in close-up with long shots of the surrounding nature, indifferent to human suffering.

One could read *The Fortress* as a more introspective philosophical drama than an action-filled war film. As King Injo vacillates between fighting with honor till death or giving into the enemy's demands to save his subjects, his two chief ministers passionately debate. Once again, Hwang stages an internal psychic conflict: the discord between honorable resistance and pragmatic compromise personified by Minister Kim Sang-heon and Minister Choe Myung-gil, respectively. A practical thinker who prioritizes people's well-being over ideological doctrine, Choe implores the king with reason: "There is nothing the strong can't do to the weak. Likewise, there is nothing the weak wouldn't do to survive. . . . Death cannot be endured, but humiliation can be endured." Ever an uncompromising idealist, Kim responds with a staunch principle: "Life in humiliation is worse than death." Choe's practical resilience and Kim's principled stubbornness might never see each other eye to eye, but the director's vision behind it deploys a flexible and complementary fusion of the two opposite extremes which eventually merge. "I saw myself drawn to both Choe Myung-gil and Kim Sang-heon,"[6] Hwang acknowledged in an interview, presenting how the twin brothers in *Silenced* evolved into ideological halves that constitute a national whole. Hwang differs from conventional morality plays by playing both sides. He's more interested in the process of debate than its outcome, and his productive deployment of twin figures again ties to the way Gi-hun and Sang-woo were shaped in *Squid Game*.

Much like *Squid Game*, *The Fortress* ends with the birth of a new family emerging from battleground ashes. Those who lost their biological family forge new family ties. A war orphan girl is adopted by the war's hero, foreshadowing brighter days to come where common folks may live in peace. When the deadly competitions conclude in *Squid Game*, the deceased Player 067's little brother will become a new child figure for the deceased Player 218's mother. Hwang rejoices in redemption via an unlikely pairing. Even more, both *The Fortress* and *Squid Game* were produced by Siren Pictures under the stewardship of the chief producer Kim Ji-yeon and the same actors appear in both productions: Cho Ah-in, Ga-yeong (Player 456's daughter) in *Squid Game*, is the orphaned girl in *The Fortress*; Lee

Byung-hun, *Squid Game*'s Front Man, is Choe Myung-gil in *The Fortress*; and Heo Sung-tae, who plays *Squid Game*'s most notorious gangster Deok-su, is the Manchu general in *The Fortress*. Working with these actors in *The Fortress* must have given the director an insight into how they might be cast in *Squid Game*.

During his hiatus between *The Fortress* and *Squid Game*, Hwang supported his former assistant director Park Jung-bae by producing and writing the script of *Collectors* (*Dogul*, 2020), which Park directed. Just like the shift from *Silenced* to *Miss Granny*, Hwang once again leaped from the somber to the ridiculous. A conventional heist movie, *Collectors* showcases Hwang's fondness for comedy thrillers with cartoonish characters, and one can see wisps of that comedy in *Squid Game*. Ever chimeric in his choice of genre and subject matter, Hwang refuses to calcify into a single aesthetic, and *Squid Game* benefits from his willingness to dabble, to paint with all sorts of tonal and cinematic colors.

THE PRODUCTION TEAM

Hwang's multifocal vision demanded similarly versatile design, and he found his match in Chae Kyoung-sun, the artistic director of *Squid Game*. Chae's appetite for challenge ("I have urge to try out new genres all the time")[7] makes her a perfect teammate for Hwang. It's no wonder the two collaborated on many productions prior to *Squid Game*. Chae is the daughter of two cinephiles who had a formative influence on her career choice. After majoring in set design in college, she found work as an assistant art director for multiple film productions. Her debut as chief set designer came in 2010 with the indie film *Come, Closer* (*Jogeumman deo gakkai*), but the films that made her a notable figure were period costume dramas with rich tapestries and ebullient color palettes. *Detective K: Secret of the Virtuous Widow* (*Joseon myeong-tam-jeong*, 2011) brought Chae her first Golden Bell Award (the most prestigious film award in Korea) in film design. A crime comedy set in the eighteenth-century Joseon, it showcases a broad spectrum of Chinese and Korean garments against the backdrop of a fantastical set, its interior depth created by a feast of lights and shadows. The film creates a conceptual maze where completely enclosed space looks like nature. Picture a dark aquarium where faint daylight passes through a water tank, illuminating swarming fish and casting luminous shadows onto silver-, violet-, and mauve-shaded costumes. Such inside/outside sets also occur in *Squid Game*, with the walls painted like a field and sky during the red light, green light game.

The Royal Tailor (*Sang-eui-won*, 2015), another period film, brought Chae her second Golden Bell. Here, Chae's balance between restrained and outlandish fully blossoms. A fictional story, again set in the Joseon dynasty, the film centers on a rivalry between two royal tailors with drastically different styles. Like Mozart and Salieri, one is a less gifted traditionalist while the other is an iconoclastic genius. Their sartorial creations take center stage, even in a film filled with lustrous palace chambers, dressing rooms, and banquet halls.

Between these two period films, Chae collaborated with Hwang on *Silenced* (2011) and *Miss Granny* (2013). While *Miss Granny* presents a colorful set design much similar to—albeit not as grotesque as—the one we see in *Squid Game*, it is *Silenced* that showcases Chae's stylistic versatility, showing that she's equally capable of grim realism. Set in a dilapidated school as ominous as a prison, in *Silenced* Chae constructs a gritty world of institutionalized crime where school life equals incarceration and abuse. Her use of bathroom stalls as a place where a sexualized power relationship is brokered between an oppressor and the oppressed resurfaces in *Squid Game* with Mi-nyeo and

Deok-su's bathroom tryst. She also thinks about power's relationship to surveillance. While Chae conceals the cameras in *Silenced* above the mirrored ceiling, she leaves the ones in *Squid Game* exposed and visible to the prisoners. Both choices disempower the subjects, who never get to play the role of voyeur.

After the success of *The Royal Tailor*, Chae rejoined Hwang on *The Fortress*, their third collaboration. Although set in Korea's historical past, *The Fortress* is a summation of Chae's vision—a plexus of the dark and the light, the restricted and the exuberant. The perfusion of a harsh palette over an indifferent natural landscape reverberates in *Squid Game*, which, in many ways, is an inversion of *The Fortress*. If *The Fortress* projects human suffering in achromatic bleakness, then in *Squid Game*, anguish screams in pink, green, lavender, and blue.

Chae claims her design philosophy is to "faithfully execute the holistic vision and integrity of the production rather than overwhelm it with overpowering visual effects."[8] She defines the production designer's job as to "visualize the script," but confesses that "neither much directions nor details for design were to be found in the script of *Squid Game*."[9] The empty space for imagination to flourish motivated her to "think about what would happen if the set itself became a character."[10] Her intention to animate the set by making a clear departure from the conventional design of survival thrillers matched the director's vision as well. According to Hwang,

> I have never had as many meetings about production design and costumes for a project as I did for *Squid Game*. We started out with very vague ideas for production design, including the sets, so there was a lot of blank space to fill, so to speak. I had to work with the production designer and the costume designer to fully develop those ideas. We were initially a bit conservative because survival games are usually set in a very dark and hostile environment. Often the setting feels like a prison. . . . But *Squid Game* revolves around games for children. The story started from the idea of having these childhood games. So the sets had to be aligned with the premise. *Squid Game* was conceived by rich VIPs in the world of the series designed and built by Il-nam. Much like an exhibition space. I thought that the space must look fun and exciting. I did not think the VIPs would enjoy watching the games set in a

gloomy background. And it occurred to me that they must have designed a space that was exciting to watch.[11]

Hwang and Chae's shared vision materialized through a long and laborious collaborative process, with Chae at times spending "a month or two to build just one set."[12] Her imagination, meticulous research, and execution received a deserved accolade: the 26th Art Directors Guild Award in the One Hour Contemporary Single-Camera Series category and the 74th Emmy Award in the Outstanding Production Design for a Narrative Contemporary Program (One Hour or More) for the sixth episode of *Squid Game*, "Gganbu."

Chae's kaleidoscopic set design became fully animated by composer Jung Jae-il's similarly versatile sound design. According to Chae, "the music was composed after all the sets had been built," and she did not directly converse with music director Jung.[13] But Hwang's overarching directorial vision found an ideal soundscape to match the idiosyncratic set. In recounting the experience of collaborating with Jung, Hwang shares their common ground of attention to detail and deviation from conventions:

I spent a lot of time at Jae-il's studio listening to his scores and discussing every single detail of the soundtrack. . . . He produced so many musical pieces that went beyond my imagination. Whenever I mentioned that something was a little off about a piece, he would create something completely new for me to check out. But Jae-il would often transform a score into something entirely different.[14]

Jung's chimeric musicality is due to his extensive career in all areas of music production. *Squid Game* was neither Jung's Netflix debut nor the first time he composed for a world-class director, yet film work came late in Jung's music career. He began at age fifteen as a bass guitar player for Han Sang-won's band. In 1999, at seventeen, he joined the funk band Gigs as a founding member and toured extensively. He's gone on to helm his own projects, producing sound for theater, film, and musicals, fluidly crossing over into traditional Korean music, jazz, classical music, even collaborating with the first generation of K-pop artists, such as BoA and Gangta, who were commercially successful throughout Asia in the early 2000s.

Jung also started young in film. At fifteen he was a session musician on the soundtrack of *Bad Movie* (*Nabbeun yeonghwa*, 1997) and then a keyboardist for director Hong Sangsoo's *Power of Gangwondo* (*Gangwondo-eui him*, 1998). But Jung's most notable film credit is his original soundtrack for Bong Joon-ho's Netflix-backed *Okja* (2017)—a film about a super-pig genetically modified to increase meat production, exposing the visceral suffering of animals living under hypercapitalist production and consumption. The film reaches its musical crescendo when Okja runs away from her corporate captors and enters a bustling underground arcade in Seoul, smashing all the tables, trinkets, and walls in her path. Jeong matches the chaos with an uproarious brass band, a tragicomical ambience that illustrates the turmoil caused and felt by the animal's mixture of desperation and naivety. Bong told Jung that he "wanted it to sound like a warped metal being kicked around. I [Bong] did not want this sequence to sound like a Hollywood style orchestration pouring all over you. I wanted something that is a bit amiss and a bit distorted."[15] Jung honored Bong's request by flying to Skopje, Macedonia, to record with the world-renowned brass band Dzambo Agusevi. Strongly reminiscent of Balkan-based čoček, a music and dance genre originated by Romani brass bands (its best-known cinematic adoption might be the original soundtrack of Emir Kusturica's 1995 Palme d'Or–winning *Underground*), Jung orchestrated a song of wobbling urgency, highlighting the plight of the hunted animal.

Jung finds the right sonic impression for each film sequence without feeling the need to please the director, often charting an eclectic middle ground: "Even though the director wants me to make 'red' music, the result cannot be pure red. I add my own colors to the music and it comes out in 'pink' or 'orange.'"[16] According to Jung, the compositions in *Okja* are entirely his own, as he did not want to make a film soundtrack but to produce his own music, and he played the keyboard himself.

Jung's successful collaboration with Bong continued with the Oscar-winning *Parasite* (*Gisaengchung*, 2020). Jung's international fame was minted when he juxtaposed the film's deception plot with baroque strings that echo Vivaldi or Bach. But indeed, this is Jung's own composition, high elegance undercutting the base desires rotting at the core of *Parasite*. Such a contrapuntal clash between the prim and the dirty exposes the fraud at both ends of the spectrum.

The intricate philosophy behind the composition of *Parasite* was pared down to something more rudimentary and primal in *Squid Game*. In composing the piece "Way Back Then"—now forever married to the absurd atmosphere of the show—Jung heavily relied on the recorder, the most commonly played instrument by Korean schoolchildren, as a primary instrument. He pairs the simplistic melody with a regimented single drum, potentially reminding the listeners of the march of the Prussian army. In line with this militaristic tonality, Jung himself wanted to use the 3-3-7 beat often reserved for cheerleading claps in Korean sporting events. The track accompanies the movements of the players, who, in uniform, mechanically march to their own demise. Yet the piece upends this tone in the final bars, suddenly cutting from measured recorder and drum to the sweeping strum of tremolo-drenched electric guitar, conjuring the pathos of rugged Westerns like *A Fistful of Dollars* (1964). Director Hwang also has plenty to say about this now-famous theme track:

> One of the best-known scores from the *Squid Game* soundtrack is the main theme, "Way Back Then," which used instruments like recorder flutes and castanets. I found it amazing that he could even think of something like that. When I first listened to the score, it sounded very new.

Since it was going to be the piece that opened the entire series, I asked him why he decided to create the score the way he did. He told me he created the piece by using only the musical instruments that we used to play in elementary school, because the series revolves around childhood games. To be honest with you, as much as I loved how strange and unfamiliar the music sounded, I was concerned at first that it might give the impression that *Squid Game* is a weird series. Jae-il actually had an alternative option for the main theme, which sounded more normal. So we initially decided to go with the alternative. But the original score lingered with me, and the more I thought about it, the more I liked it. I could not get it out of my head. Others agreed with me as well. In the end, instead of trying to add something that did not fit the mood of the series, which is how we chose the main theme, we decided we might as well go bold all the way, since the series itself is strange anyway.[17]

The strangeness of the sound that impressed Hwang was concocted from the hybridity of musical traditions all familiar to Jung: "I wanted it to sound like boorish Korean western, not macaroni western," he says.[18] Even within the same song, Jung employs multiple genres to evoke the bizzarro paradoxes that mark the world of *Squid Game*.

The tremolo returns on "Round I," with slow, soulful guitar strums signaling internal conflict. These haunting vibrations may evoke the cavernous soundtrack of Jim Jarmusch's *Dead Man* (1995), the musical equivalent to filling an empty stomach with well-aged whiskey. The audience's emotional response to *Squid Game* is in large part indebted to Jung's intuitive maneuvering between emotive registers with his parabolic compositions.

Perhaps the most Korean of all the tunes is "The Rope Is Tied," which underscores the tug-of-war game in the "Stick to Your Team" episode. Jung's extensive use of traditional Korean drumbeats and gongs escalate the scene's urgency, replicating the racing heartbeat of the players whose lives hang by a thread. Yet Jung matches the resolution of this hypertense scene with a liquescent guitar sound similar to "Round I," heightening the dramatic effect through contrast of both tempo and instrumentation. What has now become a ubiquitous soundscape of *Squid Game*, recognized by the billions, made Jung a global household name in film music industry, garnering him the top prize in the

TV Show/Limited Series category at the 2021 Hollywood Music in Media Awards.

But the soundtrack's breakout hit is inarguably "Pink Soldiers." As of October 2022, the song has amassed more than 8 million plays on YouTube and spawned multiple remixes.[19] Used on the show as the theme song for the pink hooded guards, the track is not by Jung, but Kim Seong-su, who goes by artistic name "23." Kim, a veteran of Korean jukebox musicals, layers both melodic and percussive choral vocals. "Pink Soldiers" tightly alternates between rapid-fire high and low pitches, producing an ominous vocalization creepy enough to be used in the *Omen* series. But on the other hand, the exclusive use of what appear to be all young female voices gives the track an air of suspense rather than pure horror. What is going to happen? As our expectations are tossed up and down with the alternating vocal pitch, we are left to wonder. This memorable sound image intensifies the mystery of the masked soldiers whose true identities we will never fully know, at least in the first season.

THE ACTORS

While Hwang, Chae, and Jung create the atmosphere, it's up to the actors to carry the show's emotional human core. Hwang cast a mix of Korean acting veterans and new faces, again creating a contrapuntal pleasure from familiarity and rawness. Arguably, the series' emotional center lies with the dyad of Oh Il-nam (Player 001) and Sung Gi-hun (Player 456). They are the first and the last players to join the games, bookending the beginning and the end of the survival journey. Both Oh Yeong-su and Lee Jung-jae, who played Oh and Sung, received nominations for the 2022 Golden Globe for Best Performance by an Actor in Supporting Roles in a Series, Limited Series, or Motion Picture Made for TV and Best Performance by an Actor in a TV Series, respectively, with Oh actually winning the award. (Lee made up for the loss a few months later by winning the Screen Actors Guild Award in Outstanding Performance by a Male Actor in a Drama Series and the Emmy Award in the Outstanding Lead Actor in a Drama Series.) Yet their careers prior to *Squid Game* unfolded very differently.

Viewers seeing Lee Jung-jae's acting for the first time in *Squid Game* may have a hard time imagining him as a leading man with conniving charisma or sexual charm. But Lee's filmography, spanning more than three decades, proves his worth as an all-around actor, having been cast in diverse roles ranging from the Korean version of Hades to an ambitious political chief of staff, from a breathtaking young rebel to a charming heist-master. However, Lee's thespian art did not always see the limelight, and he had his ups and downs throughout his long career.

Lee began as a fashion model in the early 1990s and also took several roles on TV and film, where he played true-to life characters: young, handsome, and daring. His film debut came in 1994 with *The Young Man* (*Nappeun namja*) where he starred as a struggling model hoping to make it in the industry, but his desperate gestures to fly high ended with a premature death. Although the film was critically praised, Lee's breakthrough would not arrive until his appearance in MBC TV's iconic drama *Sandglass* (1995). At that point, Lee had very little acting experience, and he was hardly given any lines, but it was this silence that impressed the audience and transformed the anonymous model into an A-list actor.

Ironically, the phenomenal success of *Sandglass* was more curse than boon for Lee. Typecast as the James Dean of Korea, his narrow range of rebellious roles did nothing to expand his acting palette. *Firebird* (*Bulsae*, 1997), for instance, featured him as a destructive conman with dreams of making it big, pretty much recycling his character in *The Young Man*. In *City of the Rising Sun* (*Taeyang-eun eopda*, 1999), he again played a young swindler, adrift and unable to find meaning. But this restless fin de siècle film, which viscerally captured his generation's precarious future, may provide *Squid Game* viewers with entertaining parallels. So many motifs resurface in *Squid Game*, as if Player 456 is a stultifying version of Lee's youthful-yet-serious character in *City of the Rising Sun.* In this 1999 film, we find Lee's twenty-five-year-old character gambling at horse tracks and extorting his mother for money out of desperation. He is also chased by loan sharks and is forced to sell his organs to pay back debt. Sound familiar? For viewers who know *City of the Rising Sun*, *Squid Game* strikes as a comic parody, now featuring a forty-six-year-old man living with his mom and still making the same mistakes.

The twenty-two-year gap between the two productions transformed Lee from a fledging youth into a middle-aged man who later shared in an interview that *City of the Rising Sun* was a turning point in his career where he discovered the joy of acting. With his role in *City of the Rising Sun*, Lee, at the age of just twenty-seven, became the youngest person to win the prestigious Blue Dragon Film Award in the Best Actor category, a record that has yet to be broken. But this honor was followed by a decade-long slump that saw neither artistic nor commercial success. Lee's rebound came only in the millennium's second decade, when he truly started to expand his filmography. In *The Face Reader* (*Gwansang*, 2013), he appeared as the king-toppling duke of the Joseon dynasty with boundless ambition. Garbed in black silk and sable fur, his tall figure formed a shady Machiavellian predator willing to do anything to quench his bloodthirsty desire for power.

In *The Maid* (2010), Lee played a young and cold-hearted entrepreneur, Hun, who makes sexual advances on a housemaid while his wife is expecting his child. Hun impregnates and abandons the maid, which leads to the maid's vengeful self-immolation in the presence of Hun's family. Playing this antihero was the turning point for Lee to truly expand his dramatic range, expertly weaving his character's external elegance with inner vulgarity. Seductively playing a grand piano while sporting a perfectly tailored suit, Hun cuts a dashing figure, yet his duplicity is fully exposed when he slurps priceless red wine, exposing his utter lack of manners. Despite the wealth and status he has come to enjoy, this paradoxical scene divulges the baseness of material luxury enjoyed by a parvenu gentleman, inviting laughter from the 63rd Cannes International Film Festival audience. This comic relief involving glugging of luxury wine resurfaces in *Squid Game* during the final banquet scene when Player 456 guzzles a glass of Romanée-Conti as if it is a bowl of kimchi stew. The stultifying effect of this tense banquet scene in *Squid Game* was produced in large part by the unconventional casting practice of director Hwang, who wanted to destroy Lee's perfect image as an actor who always played stylish and cool—albeit depraved—characters prior to his appearance in *Squid Game*.

By contrast, Oh Yeong-su is older than Lee, but because he spent most of his life in the theater world, his extensive career did not translate to celebrity or "Voice of a Generation" pressure. His half-century-long theater career started in 1963 when he joined the theater troupe Gwangjang. In 1987, he joined the government-financed National Theater Company of Korea in search of more secure employment, playing such leading roles as Dr. Faust and King Lear. In the few instances where he detoured into TV drama roles, he played short supporting parts as an inspector, a farmer, and, most prominently, a Buddhist monk. The first role as a monk, which led to his being typecast as a sage, began in 1998, but it was Oh's appearance as the old monk in Kim Ki-duk's art film *Spring, Summer, Fall, Winter and Spring* (*Bom yeoreum gaeul gyeoul geurigo bom*, 2003) that left a deep impression on moviegoers. This role led to a series of other monk roles on TV dramas, most notably as Wolcheon in the enormously popular historical drama *Queen Seondoek* (*Seondeok yeowang*, 2009). Oh played the part so convincingly that some viewers speculated he was an actual monk. A slew of monk roles followed, including *Iljimae Returns* (*Doraon Iljimae*, 2009) and *Mushin* (2012), totaling in nine appearances as a monk for TV and film productions prior to *Squid Game*. This makes Hwang's choice to cast Oh as Player 001, a character who appears monkish but later completely undermines audience expectations, even more interesting. Hwang knew Korean audiences would never suspect their favorite TV monk to be the puppet master of the games. In his late seventies, he still tries out new roles for live theater performances, such as his most recent role as Sigmund Freud in *Last Session* (*Laseuteu sesyeon*, 2022).

Just like Oh, Park Hae-soo spent years on a proscenium stage before he became active in the TV and film industry. Park's intelligent looks made him a suitable actor to play brainy characters, which led to his casting as Sang-woo in *Squid Game*. The first TV production that made him a familiar actor to a wider public was SBS's historical drama *Six Flying Dragons* (*Yuk-ryeong-i nareusha*, 2015–2016), in which Park played the sword-wielding general Yi Ji-ran, a faithful defender of the newly installed king of the Joseon dynasty. He appeared in a few more TV shows, but what garnered him the most mass popularity was a black comedy called *Prison Playbook* (*Seulgi-ro-un gambang sael-hwal*, 2018–2019). *Squid Game* was not the first time Park found himself incarcerated in a role; in *Prison Playbook* he played a baseball player who lands in prison who then forges unlikely friendships with inmates from all walks of life. Following suit was a crime comedy *By Quantum Physics: A Nightlife Venture* (*Yangja mulihak*, 2019), in which Park appeared as a nightclub hustler fighting a drug trafficking circle. The film was not well received, but Park's acting impressed the critics and public alike, garnering him the New Actor Award at the 2019 Blue Dragon Film Awards.

Squid Game marked Park's first Netflix drama appearance, which left a strong impression on the worldwide viewers with his cunning yet convincing portrayal of an antihero. Park appeared in two additional new Netflix dramas: *Suriname* (2022), a highly acclaimed thriller set in Central America where he played a South Korean officer chasing a drug trafficking ring for the National Intelligence Service. He also starred as Berlin in the flop Korean remake of the popular Spanish TV series *Money Heist*.

The true complexity of Player 218's criminal mind, masterfully depicted by Park, can only be fully accentuated by more ostentatious villains such as Doek-su and his crew. Heo Sung-tae played Player 101, the snake-tattooed gang leader whose blunt thuggishness endowed the show with a sharper edge and presented a wider gamut of human characteristics. Having majored in Russian language in college, Heo started his career as an LG Electronics employee selling flatscreen TVs in Russia. But he soon became disillusioned with the life of a salary man and—as a somewhat compulsive gamble—entered an acting contest, launching his acting career in his late thirties. In the early days, he struggled to get steady work, but gradually he built his profile as an actor specializing in villains and gangsters. In *Monster* (*Goemul*, 2021), which aired on JCTB TV, he made good use of his college major, cursing tastefully in Russian at critical moments, adding a fine-tuned detail to his racketeer character. His exception to being typecast as a criminal came with director Hwang's film *The Fortress*, where Heo played a Qing general who spoke exclusively in the Manchu language. For this role, Heo underwent extensive Manchu lessons and honed his pronunciation. Compared to the seedy swindler and punch man roles Heo usually plays, this character had a much more dignified air. Still, it will be interesting to follow Heo's future career with an eye on whether he can break out of such stereotypically molded roles.

Discussion of Deok-su, Player 101, would be incomplete without Han Mi-nyeo, Player 212, who later goes down on the glass bridge with her protector-turned-nemesis. Played by veteran actor Kim Joo-ryung, Player 212 shows us that at the bottom of all her self-serving calculations, survival instinct and extreme vulnerability loom large. Kim's filmography is as versatile as those of director Hwang and Lee Jung-jae; her roles range from a chillingly malicious school staffer in *Silenced* to a hysterical aunt in the tiger mom saga *SKY Castle* (2018–2019). Hwang's experience working with Kim on *Silenced* convinced him to cast her in *Squid Game*. She has appeared mostly in short film roles, including such notable productions as Bong Joon-ho's *Memories of Murder* (*Sal-in-eui cho-eok*, 2003). Although she has acted for TV for only five years, she's scored roles in several critically acclaimed productions, including *Mr. Sunshine* (*Miseuteo syeonshain*, 2018). Although she does not play leading roles, Kim is a mood maker, helping to find the subtle tonality for the productions in which she appears. Her presence feels weighty and visceral, making her a perfect ensemble actor for *Squid Game*.

While these actors are well-established figures in Korean entertainment industry, Hwang made a bet on relatively new faces to strike a balance between familiarity and newness. Of all newcomers on set, Jung Ho-yeon played the most significant role, Gang Sae-byeok, Player 067, one of the three standing survivors in the aftermath of the penultimate game. Trained as a professional model, Jung was in New York preparing for Fashion Week when her agency asked her to fly back to Korea to audition for the show. Hwang wanted an unknown actor for the role of Sae-byeok and was impressed with Jung, casting her immediately. Who would have predicted back then that this complete novice would go onto win the 2022 SAG Award in Outstanding Performance by a Female Actor in a Drama Series? *Squid Game* was Jung's drama debut, but her memorable performance as the North Korean defector made her an audience favorite, igniting a bright future as a Korean drama and film star.

The best ensemble acting scene in *Squid Game* could arguably be the Player 067 and Player 240 scene in episode 6, "Gganbu." Lee Yoo-mi played the apathetic Player 240, who exited the games through voluntary death, partially because she felt no reason to live and partially to support the cause of her newfound friend. In a show featuring so many cutthroat, opportunistic men, the scene stands out as beautifully generous and self-sacrificial. Player 240 is the only known player who joined the game in order to die, not to live, and she draws out Jeong's largely silent and brooding character, finally revealing the reasons for her reserved nature to the audience. Faced with death, Lee both tears up and smiles broadly. She captures the full paradox of life without reason, or existence without substratum, in just a few seconds. Her presence, because it's so fleeting, reverberates as both tragic and celebratory.

Unlike her novice acting partner Jung, Lee is a veteran performer of TV and films since age fifteen. Viewers of K-drama may remember Lee as a self-harming patient suffering from Munchausen syndrome in the MBC TV drama *365: Repeat the Year* (2020). The premise of *365: Repeat the Year* consists of the characters' participation in a mysterious yet deadly game. No wonder Player 240 looked so relaxed and unaffected in *Squid Game*; she's (fictionally) been here before. The work that cemented Lee's status as a serious actor was her appearance in the indie film *Park Hwa-yeong* (2017) and its sequel *Young Adult Matters* (*Eo-reun-deul-eun molayo*, 2020). In this arresting exposé of the drifting lives of runaway youths, she appears as a tittering teenage girl bullied by her classmates and impregnated by her teacher. The film spirals into harsh psychological territory when Lee's character decides to abort the pregnancy. Her vacuous glance and dry tone of speech in these scenes—as if nothing matters anymore—likely shaped Lee's portrayal of the nihilistic character traits of Player 240, for which she became the first Korean actor to win an Emmy (in the category of Outstanding Guest Actress).

An equally refreshing new face in *Squid Game* was Anupam Tripathi. Like Lee, he brought lively energy to the ensemble. Born in New Delhi in 1988, Tripathi was a part of the playwright Shahid Anwar's Behroop theater group from 2006 to 2010. Hoping to expand his acting skills, he came to Korea in 2010 on a scholarship to study at the Korean National University of Arts. Upon graduation, he took many small roles as immigrant laborers or criminals from Nepal, Sri Lanka, and Pakistan, typecast as a foreigner, a trend that continues in *Squid Game*. Tripathi's debut film came in 2014 with the film *Ode to My Father* (*Gukje sijang*, 2014), a commercial success that attracted 10 million viewers. Tripathi appeared as a Sri Lankan factory worker who speaks in Busan accent, only to face ridicule by a group of South Korean teenagers. The typecasting that started with *Ode to My Father* continued, since there still is a conspicuous lack of nuanced characters given to non-Korean actors in Korean productions. In this regard, Tripathi has spoken about his surprise when he received the script for *Squid Game* and it included another foreign migrant laborer role, but this time with extensive character development.

Although *Squid Game* is Tripathi's breakthrough performance, it's not his first time on Netflix. The first was *Space Sweepers* (*Seung-ri-ho*, 2021), a dystopian space opera set in a completely deforested earth in 2092. Tripathi plays the English-speaking secretary of a genius scientist who creates a celestial paradise for refugees escaping the uninhabitable earth. He then went onto narrating the Sanskrit prologue in *The Eighth Night* (*Je pal-il-eui bam*, 2021). Fluent in Hindi, English, and Korean, he has great potential to expand his acting opportunities, especially now that the world has seen his ability to portray a highly empathetic character like Player 199.

Any television production brings together a wide array of voices. It is an inherently collaborative medium, especially when working with a veteran director at the production level of *Squid Game*. But here, Hwang achieved alchemy by truly synthesizing his many skill sets and influences to create a blend that draws from, but is completely different than, his previous work. He assembled some actors known for drama and some for comedy, along with a composer who can write for European string quartets, traditional Korean drums, and American electric guitar.

He gave Chae, his designer, new challenges, playing off her expertise in both the lavish and the grimy. His actors play against type, in the case of Lee, and with type, as with Oh and Tripathi, and he found a new depth for them inside the life-or-death stakes of *Squid Game*. It's a show of wildly vacillating tones, and in some ways it's simultaneously Hwang's most violent *and* most family-friendly mainstream drama yet. *Squid Game* works *because* of its contradictions. Here, versatility is an asset, not a hinderance. Hwang and his crew made a niche show that found a massive audience, eager to veer off to uncharted territory where they take vicarious risks in order to win it all.

2

PLAY AT YOUR OWN RISK

The pandemic era has arrived. Through the birth canal of horror and despair, it has brought about the simultaneous sense of a new beginning and an imminent end. More than three years into this new epoch, where do we find ourselves in this world? What is at stake? Putting our ears closer to the heartbeat of today, we hear symptoms of our times in recurring sound waves and visions: filled with tension and crisis, an eschatological view of the world emerges, warning us of the precarity of human life, the ethics of medicine, and the ubiquitous presence of surveillance mechanisms, all mitigated by the horrors and wonders of technology.

Without the pandemic, what would our perception of *Squid Game* have been like? *Squid Game* is, among many other things, a pandemic-age opera, where risk taking and crisis, like shapeshifting villains, sing duets in endless variations. They might not be identical twins but first cousins. After all, what is crisis other than the unfolding of miscalculated risks? The enormity of the crises in our times forges various entanglements: one's crisis might be another's opportunity, or one's calamity—in an extremely perverse fashion—might be another's entertainment.

As a millennial parable on the pandemic, *Squid Game* speaks of the impossibility of free choice, the futility of human willpower, and the uneven rise of new cultural networks brought about by ever-intensifying global streaming wars. Risk-taking by the show's characters and viewers alike signals the pressing symptoms of the current era, when digital transformations and accelerated sociopolitical changes have been compressed to intensify the stakes of our everyday lives. What made *Squid Game* a fresh wheel to spin a time-proven story of money, death, and family is the extraordinary risks ordinary people take every day. One risk averted, and we've survived another day. But how many more minutes and seconds will our luck last?

TIME BOMB

Have you ever seen time detonate? It takes the shape of a million dust motes in the air. Eternally suspended in slow motion, time scatters like mist from a fountain across vast emptiness, undoing our usual sense of temporal metrics, turning seconds into eternity. When the last second ticks off in the penultimate stepping-stone game, we literally see how one second becomes protracted into fifty-four seconds: the glass bridge shatters into crystal-like debris, slowly scuffing the three surviving contestants' faces.[1] What can this nearly frozen time bomb express?

Squid Game lacks the poetic tonality of Lars von Tier's *Melancholia* (2011), but it may inadvertently be paying homage to that film's unforgettable opening sequence in which the world is set on a fatal collision course. The vision of the impending apocalypse is made ever more unbearable by its eternal prolonging of time. With the exceptions of tug-of-war and squid game, every contest in *Squid Game* unfolds to the suspenseful ticking of a stopwatch. To capture the maximal pressure of running out of time, the screen time often exceeds the actual time limit allocated to each game. The first game, red light, green light, takes place within a five-minute period but is doubled in screen time to capture the heightened horror and struggle of the contestants. Honeycomb, a ten-minute game, takes up seventeen minutes of screen time, throwing both contestants and viewers into a pressure cooker simmering with suspense and fear. Marble game must end in thirty minutes, but a staggering forty minutes of screen time is allocated to it, practically an entire episode. Stepping-stone is set up with a ten-minute limit, but the sense of time is extended so that the viewers feel eternally trapped in the moment of tormenting choice between two identical-looking glasses. At the fork between life and death, survival and extinction, the bridge crossers halt, and we even hear their rapid heartbeats against the cold mechanical ticking sound of a stopwatch.

The sounds of deep psychological horror and thrill emanate from the nonchalant countdown of a time bomb, signaling the collision between the inescapable end and the desire to live. Episode 6, "Gganbu," captures that eerie dissonance most viscerally: the cold, faceless digital clock displays ticking seconds against the blazing sky, painfully highlighting the slippage of time (see figure on the following page). Under the simmering pressure, the gaming arena turns into a petri dish where viewers can examine each player's true colors under a magnifying glass. This is where the first and the last player, Gi-hun and Il-nam, forge a fatal partnership in a cutthroat elimination game. Seeing his life slipping away with every wasted second, Gi-hun rushes—and threatens—the distracted Il-nam to play the game. The urgent rawness

In the sixth episode "Gganbu," friends and foes must bring an end to their relationship as the digital stopwatch ticks away like a timebomb. NETFLIX

of the moment expressed through the blazing dusk, however, is met with a strange artificial counterforce. The sky is far from natural, but merely a painted indoor panel displaying the equally artificial white neon digits of an oversized clock. Under this grotesque scenery, for the first time, our Everyman Gi-hun turns dark, resorting to deception to survive and win. He does not have mental space to reflect upon the cruel irony here: that rushing to play the game is rushing to his own potential death.

But Gi-hun's unfortunate partner, Il-nam, is no stranger to such harsh rules. As the chief architect of all the games, Il-nam invites Gi-hun to play the last game of his life in the final episode. He is no longer that sweet old man awkwardly placed in the deadly arena, soiling his pants and kindly letting others have the upper hand. We meet Il-nam at his deathbed, but even in his vulnerable state, he appears a coldhearted puppeteer who toys with people's lives for the entertainment of the rich. Equally harsh and pessimistic, Il-nam, in his last game, bets on the life of a homeless man on the frosty street, on the scenario that no one will come to rescue the man before midnight. Unlike in the previous games, where he could bail out with a fake death, this time Il-nam's own life is also at stake. Whether he loses or wins, he knows perfectly well he will expire soon. In the first episode, he tells Gi-hun he suffers from a brain tumor, pointing to his head as if it is a time bomb. A reminder that death is lurking in close proximity, a close-up of the clock's hands by Il-nam's bedside marks the end of the time. Whether he placed his bet correctly or not, the game's ending takes his life away, illustrating that nobody, even the greatest manipulator of human fate, can reverse the course of time.

The absolute tyranny of time running down to the unavoidable destination of death rules over all the games, even those that do not come with a nominal time limit. Although tug-of-war and squid game are not strictly limited, we see the time bomb ticking away with characters' increasing physical exhaustion that leaves wear and tear on their bodies. In the absence of an actual watch, the body becomes a stopwatch, with wounds and scars marking the passage of time in these episodes. We see the blisters on the palms of tug-of-war players degenerate into torn skin and deep stabs in the final squid game—the game that can come to an end only with a fatal wound to the body. The slowing heartbeat of those who lost is the stopwatch that signals the end.

The sound of the ticking clock spills out of the gaming arena and soon dominates the entire drama, merging with the palpitation of agitated hearts. Think of episode 5, where the bankrupt doctor-cum–Player 111 rushes to his forbidden operation. Navigating the darkened maze of corridors and stairs, he reaches a room where he will lift out organs from the dead players. The freshness of the harvested organs depends on how much time has elapsed since the victim's death, turning the human bodies into the marker of time.

A time bomb is an intuitive allegory to address today's existential crises, entangled networks where it is nearly impossible to tell the beginning from the end or the cause from the effect. While they all screech in a simultaneous cacophony, one register stands out: a denunciation of capitalist time characterized by a limitless expansion and a dramatic bust. With each second's passing, capital should grow and gain, and we should welcome the accumulation of debt so long as the borrowed capital will yield enough to pay off the principal and generate some profit. Here, risk-taking becomes a virtue—even a necessary prerequisite for a big windfall.

But boundless greed cannot swell forever. When Gi-hun goes to a hair salon in the final episode, the camera captures the news program on TV somberly reporting that South Korea's household debt is the second fastest-growing in the world. Although presented in a brief, passing manner, this pivotal detail marks the critical passage of Gi-hun's transformation into a new being (visually marked by the brand-new red color of his hair). Almost a moment of cinema verité, the salon sequence confronts viewers with the documentarian truth of South Korea's economic crisis simmering in the timed pressure cooker on the verge of explosion. Actual Korean media literally refer to the danger of an increasing debt as a "time bomb." The various reasons each player joined the deadly games on the show are all too realistic: as for many real-life debtors, gambling and risk-taking might be more appealing to *Squid Game*'s contestants than succumbing to the tyranny of the inevitable bust and demise. For Gi-hun, sitting in the hair salon, the burden stems from the sense of indebtedness to other contestants for their sacrifice rather than the financial debt. Even if he is financially free now as the winner of the games, he cannot be guilt free, making him a de facto dead person.

Faced with the vision of their own extinction, everyone turns to gambling in an attempt to either escape or challenge—and perhaps reverse—the course of their fate. Just as nobody can avoid the end of the games, this desperate gesture seems to apply to people of all walks of life. Those without the basic means to sustain a livelihood may gamble compulsively in any forms accessible, but people with substantial means do the same out of boredom. The VIPs who later arrive at the island to watch the deadly games as entertainment bet on human lives, and it is their gambling that enables the entire premise of the yearly tournaments.

Who else is addicted to gambling? What about Ali's boss? Although he hasn't paid Ali in six months, we catch him in the middle of gambling online when Ali bursts into his office to demand his unpaid wages. But no one is as hopeless as Gi-hun, a compulsive gambler thirsty

Gi-hun's deep financial desperation leads him to procure his daughter's birthday present at an arcade claw machine.
ALBUM / ALAMY STOCK PHOTO

for instant gratification, going so far as to steal from his mother. With no money to buy his only daughter's birthday present after losing it all at a horse track, the desperate father dives into small-scale gambling, trying his luck with an arcade claw machine (see figure above).

The addiction is so overpowering that even highly rational and calculating Sang-woo gambles with his clients' money, investing in futures under the delusion that they will yield him a huge gain. Upon being released from the island after the first game, Sang-woo runs into Gi-hun and tells him the extent of his loss, totaling nearly $6 million (US).

Sang-woo: I dealt in futures.

Gi-hun: Futures? You bet that much on a gift? What kind of gift was it for you to risk that much money? Was there a girl involved?

Sang-woo: It's not that kind of a gift.

The show plays with the Korean homonym *seon-mul*, which means both "futures" and "gift" (as will be illustrated in the following chapter, the gift is associated with death), presenting a cruel joke about how both are adulterated by the destructive gambling mentality. Hwang comments on the centrality of gambling, as it has become a part of today's way of being, and how climate change and the appearance of crypto- and virtual currency have made the idea of *Squid Game* more authentic:

> [It's] almost like a lottery now—almost like a gamble where people in reality have actually doubled or really increased their wealth overnight. And I feel like the world is gradually moving toward dystopia. There are more and more people who really don't dream about the future, and that drives people to want to gamble, to really

take it all and put it all on the line and hope for the best. And I think these changes have created an environment where the idea of people putting their life on the line playing children's games is no longer something that is too absurd.[2]

With every ticking second, children's games and deadly gambles become almost indistinguishable. At the end point where the two completely fuse, our Everyman Gi-hun is treated to a rude awakening. Sitting with the Front Man in a limousine, about to be dropped off to the streets he came from, blindfolded Gi-hun confronts the Front Man: "Who are you? Who are you all? Why do those things?" Sipping champagne, the Front Man responds nonchalantly, "You like horse race, don't you? You are like horses in a race." This brutally honest diagnosis of how some human lives have turned into mere cogs in a large gambling machine penetrates deeply into Gi-gun's consciousness. It festers there so badly that he turns away from a plane trip to see his daughter in Los Angeles to confront the masterminds of the games. His last words staunchly deny the underlying causes of today's crisis: "I am not a horse. I am a human."

So the games go on.

FRONT MAN VERSUS EVERYMAN

Gi-hun's awakening is a long time coming. His decision to participate in the games and gamble everything pays off in the end, but at what human price? (see figure below). What shocks viewers is not just the gory depiction of violence but the premise: an antithesis to Jeremy Bentham's greatest happiness principle. Instead of attempting to please the majority, the games are designed to allow just

Gi-hun is presented like a cog in a huge machinery, or a product in a warehouse. According to production designer Chae, the inspiration for the dormitory design came from visiting a warehouse store, which made her wonder: "What if there are humans instead of products?" Zoom interview with the author, May 31, 2022. ALBUM / ALAMY STOCK PHOTO

one contestant to survive and thrive at the price of the rest. But that lone survivor does not live happily ever after; otherwise, where would be the element of drama? Actor and comedian Bill Irwin once said, "Drama is a character with a problem,"[3] and the true drama of *Squid Game* lies in how the survivor, Gi-hun, ended up far from happy. This is where the Front Man's mystery looms large. He was once Gi-hun himself, a lone survivor standing on the heap of dead competitors. How did he get to where he is now—not just finding composure to move on but even going farther to take a major role in perpetuating the institution that created him in the first place?

Of countless attributes that separate the Front Man from our Everyman Gi-hun, the most conspicuous is his intriguing face covering. For nearly all the episodes, viewers never get to see the face of the Front Man behind his signature polygonic mask. The intricate facade layered with angles adds mystery to this chief enabler of the deadly institution: his motivation, his origins, his aspirations and dark dreams are all concealed behind its thickness (see figure on the following page).

The unknowability of risk-taking, gambling, and the ensuing crises becomes literalized in the masks of *Squid Game*. Masks primarily shield the faces of those in power,

Front Man stands out with his unique polygonic mask.
MOVIESTORE COLLECTION / ALAMY STOCK PHOTO

making it easy for the guards, the Front Man, and the VIPs to conceal both their accountability and any traces of humanity or empathy they might feel for the players. Just as each game has a simple but strict set of rules, the use of masks follows one straight logic: if you take the mask off, you will become vulnerable—and most likely perish.

It is the Front Man who announces this rule loud and clear for everyone to hear. When a failed contestant in the honeycomb game faces execution, out of desperation, he grabs a gun and threatens a guard to take his mask off. From behind that impersonal shield emerges the fresh face of a young man barely in his mid-twenties. But the revelation of a human face quickly goes punished by the Front Man, who shoots the unmasked guard for having revealed his identity. The same fate is reserved for another guard who operates a secret organ trafficking ring: as soon as he takes off his mask, a bullet enters his body. It is the Front Man who pulls the trigger again. So when the Front Man voluntarily takes his mask off to reveal his bare face to his brother, he fully understands how this exposure will make him vulnerable.

Bare faces equal exposure to danger, as all contestants' faces are uncovered and clearly display fear, desperation, and resignation. Gi-hun is a case in point. As the clock ticks off seconds in the honeycomb game, he wrestles to increase his odds of survival by licking the back side of his umbrella-shaped candy. A close-up shot reveals more than his face at this critical moment. An extremely intimate view of his pores, his birthmark, and the protruding arteries on his neck exposes him so much, we feel we can almost smell his sweaty fear and raw vulnerability.

Like a miasma, fear spreads in the air for those unmasked. The fear of ticking time is compounded by the fear of contagion. During the red light, green light game, we see a woman holding her face, screaming hysterically. Her bare skin is spattered with the blood of a fellow contestant who has just been shot. In the moment, her shock turns into a piercing shriek and a physical convulsion that gets her shot as a result. This horrid scene—often compared to Edvard Munch's *The Scream* by many fans of the show—presents an absurdly accurate scene in the age of COVID-19, when the fusing of bodily fluids may literally result in death.

The horror of this moment is compounded by the unmasked subjects being slammed en masse into an enclosed indoor space. Upon the shocking conclusion of the red light, green light game, the outdoor field turns into an indoor arena with an automatic sliding roof. According to Hwang, the set was inspired by Sin City, which itself is a prime site of manufacturing fakery. "We drew some inspiration from hotels in Las Vegas. . . . You know those hotels that have fake skies drawn on the ceiling? I wanted to create a space that made people wonder, 'Is that fake or real?'" says Hwang. "So you'll see in the first game, we actually mixed a fake sky with a real one."[4] Here, the confusion between the fake and the real translates into the confusion between indoors and outdoors, making those without masks feel ever more subject to the risk of contamination. The large, windowless dormitory for contestants where an unmasked 456 people breathe the same air induces the same degree of fear, as do the vans that bring contestants to the island, where masked guard drivers stay sober while the unmasked recruits soon pass out.

Masks have become the new face of the pandemic and arguably reveal more than they conceal. The protected faces of the Front Man and the VIPs are no exceptions to these rules. The beast-shaped half masks for VIPs are more theatrically curious than menacing, and their eccentric shapes draw more attention to their faces—and their bestial nature—than covering them. The masks are covered with shiny glass mosaic pieces and glimmer under the decadent amber light. It is a strange connection to the shattering glass bridge—a cruel spectacle for VIPs to enjoy from below, wearing the masks covered with glass pieces. The subject and object of the gaze here completely fuse, giving birth to a crisis of perception.

In *Squid Game*, the circular connection between the masked and the unmasked also revolves around the practice of surveillance—another key aspect of life under COVID. At first glance, those who are masked have the power to surveil. First there are masked guard soldiers who surveil the barefaced contestants. Then there are managerial guards who surveil the contestants as well as the guard soldiers. Then there are combat guards with automatic machine guns who execute those defying the rules of mask wearing. Finally, there is the Front Man, who supervises them all.

Front Man's multi-angled mask is a set of multiple sur-veilling eyes embodied. The many surfaces seem to indi-cate that he can see everything from every angle. The Front Man is often shown in his plush private lounge resembling an executive viewing room. The show's viewers are often invited to watch the games through his surveilling gaze, as he is comfortably seated in a lounge chair facing an over-sized screen while the drama of life and death unfolds there in real time. The act of surveillance here is nothing short of leisure and luxury, as we can glean from how the Front Man watches red light, green light. As the constant automatic gunshots turn the playground into a mass killing field, the masked supervisor is removed from the immediacy of the violence. The Front Man's surveillance is made even more enjoyable by a languid vocal performance of a light jazz song, "Fly to the Moon," crisscrossing with the constant firing of machine guns, once again producing a grotesque rhythm and sound that couple horror and entertainment.

On the receiving end of surveillance, however, there is only horror. At first, the contestants are too shell-shocked to realize they are being monitored by the forces determining their fate. But soon, the first contest tells them clearly that a huge part of the game is about being watched on every step of their journey. Even before the games begin, we witness how the convenient surveillance mechanism becomes a prerequisite as the drugged contestants are smuggled to an island. Everyone then has a chip planted behind their ear for quick identification and facile monitoring. The policeman who sneaks onto the island in search of his missing brother is the only exception. Even when the winners leave at the end of the games, unbeknownst to them, they will carry the chip in their bodies and be followed by an all-surveilling eye. No wonder Il-nam knows exactly what Gi-hun has been up to since his release. So does the Front Man, who tells Gi-hun to board the plane to LA in the final scene. Has he been watching Gi-hun on a large screen in his plush lounge all this time? Let's not forget that the games have been staged since 1988, but the world out there knows nothing of it, with the winners maintaining silence in the face of omniscient surveillance machinery.

Intensified surveillance of individuals through temperature monitoring and contact tracing have become an intrinsic ritual of the COVID era, and *Squid Game*'s appeal to a broad cross-cultural audience beyond Korea speaks to how we can easily discern the allegories of surveillance. Surveillance applies to all. Nobody seems to escape it in this day and age. But is it really an equalizing force? Can it be hijacked as a tool to intensify the deepening inequality even further?

EQUALITY AND FAIRNESS FOR ALL?

One sign of what makes *Squid Game* a pandemic drama is its pronounced obsession with the question of equality. Long before COVID, the ever-broadening wealth gap became endemic to most societies, but it has intensified further during the pandemic era. Even the shape of recovery from COVID has primarily benefited the wealthy, while those who struggled economically remain in precarious positions. In today's deeply bifurcated world, how much do the top 1 percent actually interact with ordinary folks, other than occasional encounters with their house cleaners, gardeners, and drivers? Can people with different origins and life experiences stay in the same room without decimating one another?

Squid Game explores the pressing questions of today's social divide by throwing people from all walks of life in a condensed pressure-cooker environment. The island is a test lab to experiment and observe how contestants with diverse backgrounds react to one another. This was precisely the director's concern when arranging a potpourri of humankind: "If you look at the cast of characters, you have the elite member of the society, Sang-woo. You have the blue-collar, middle-class man, Gi-hun. You have the migrant worker, Ali. You have Sae-byeok and you have Il-nam, who sort of represents the senior class. They may seem very specific to Korea, but I think they constitute the minority in any country in the world."[5] Indeed, Ali is an immigrant worker from Pakistan who is also disabled. Sae-byeok is a North Korean resettler in South Korea, having to provide for her little brother while planning to bring her parents out of North Korea. Il-nam is a senior with signs of dementia, unable to care for himself. All of them are part of what South Korean society as a whole has come to mark as the subaltern minority.

But the director's comment leaves out a crucial detail: that Il-nam, one of the top 1 percent, is also in the mix masquerading as socially weak. The disguise heightens the spirit of social experiment and maximizes the irony of the test lab created by 456 players. In a microcosmos where cliques emerge and individuals clash, one thing remains clear for all: everyone in delusional hope tries to become the front man, but deep down they know too well that the rules of the games do not allow for such a utopia to exist.

Contrary to every participant's intuitive understanding of the inequality, the game organizers emphasize the importance of fairness and equal opportunity to a great extent. The synthetic voice of the guard, in a measured tone, repeatedly emphasizes that the rules apply fairly to all and that everyone will have an equal chance to participate in the games. With the suggestion of voting, the perverse act of staging equal opportunity begins. Sang-woo brings up the players' collective bargaining rights when the survivors of the red light, green light game hope to quit: "Clause three of the consent form: the games may be terminated upon a majority vote." Out of the fair spirit that has been emphasized all along, the guards acknowledge the clause; following the democratic principle of the majority vote, every participant casts their vote to decide whether to continue with the games or bail out and return to their hopeless lives (see figure on the following page).

But this is hardly a fair election. At best, it is the mockery of it, since the rules are deeply rigged by Il-nam's presence. He is the one who had the choice between watching the games as the VIP spectator or temporarily descending to the bottom of the social pit for amusement

Contestants are given a chance to vote whether to continue with the deadly games. ALBUM / ALAMY STOCK PHOTO

and thrills. ("Watching the games cannot be more interesting than doing the games.") Il-nam knows all too well that other players simply cannot afford such a luxury but have to continue with the games, even fully knowing the consequences. Casting a final vote to discontinue, he first releases the contestants into the world, only to make them return voluntarily to their own graveyard. The broached rules of fairness do not go unnoticed by the players either. When Player 119 is about to be eliminated upon losing the honeycomb game, he confronts the guards: "What kind of sick game is this? Why do some get an easy shape when others are stuck with difficult ones?"

The emphasized principle of equality and fairness become a moot point once more when the secret organ trade ring is discovered and punished for their violation of the fairness rule. A few guards who profit from having access to dead—or nearly dead—bodies of failed contestants recruit a doctor among the players to join an organ trafficking ring. When the ring is discovered by the Front Man, he attempts to straighten out the rules by executing them all with his final verdict: "You've ruined the most crucial element of this place. Equality. Everyone is equal in these games. Players compete in a fair game under the same conditions. These people suffered from inequality and discrimination out in the world and we offer them one last chance to fight on equal footing and win. But you have broken that principle." To prove his point, the Front Man has the dead cheaters hung up in a prominent place contestants must pass through as they march to their next survival game. Accompanying the horrid scene is the synthetic voice of the organizer speaking in a polite tone: "You are witnessing the fates of those who broke the rules of this world for their own benefit and furthermore tainted the pure ideology of this world. Here you are all equal, with equal opportunity and no discrimination. We promise to prevent such misfortune from happening again. We sincerely apologize for this incident." Overemphasizing fairness and equality underscores their lack, but more crucially, could the Front Man be potentially confusing fairness with equality here?

The terms *equality* and *fairness* many be used interchangeably in everyday conversations, but closer reflection makes us realize that the former is more about creating even access to opportunity (hence "equal opportunity") whereas the latter concerns the lack of bias (hence "fair judgment"). So many idealists and revolutionaries have pursued equality, but it is a utopian ideal that may never be achieved in reality. On the other hand, fairness might be granted in games that have an unambiguous set of rules, as in *Squid Game*. The confusion happens when the organizers conflate the feasible implementation of fairness with the foundational principle of equality—the belief that all humans deserve the same degree of dignity, respect, and opportunity. To this notion, Jacques Rancière noted that equality should be the starting point, not the end point.[6] When the game organizers say "equality," what they really mean is "fairness of rules," which may not always be married to the dignity of human life: for instance, one can be fair in giving everyone the same degree of cruel punishment. By applying this logic to everyone, the games are perversely parading punitive fairness as equality. Punitive rules apply fairly to the game players and quickly become translated into equal opportunity.

But not everyone in the arena is given a fair measure, even in the flawed sense of the word *fairness*. The last to cast a vote on whether the players should bail out of the games or not is Il-nam, who has the advantage of knowing the entire flow of the games. Although everyone fairly gets one vote, great inequality exists in their knowledge, inevitably influencing the way they vote. In a similar fashion, the rules of red light, green light were not shared up front, as no contestants except Il-nam knew that failure to comply with the rules would result in death. Il-nam also has the power to stop any games with a desperate cry (as the Front Man immediately stops the nighttime slaughter when he spots the frightened Il-nam). Further, the rules of the children's games are not familiar to social outsiders like the Pakistani laborer or the North Korean resettler. Although everyone is given a fair judgment of their performance, some games benefit the physically strong (tug-of-war), others benefit those with good luck and intuition (honeycomb), while still other games benefit those with heartless cruelty and cunning (as in Sang-woo's elimination of Ali and Sae-byeok).

Despite the repeated claims about the fairness of the games, no player is so naive as to believe in the pronounced fairness. Once they realize that there are great advantages to sticking with the physically strong, a pecking order quickly is established. The games in the beginning give the impression that the physically strong have an advantage over the weak, in turn imparting a clear sense of the food chain. The meager meals served to the contestants—bread and a small carton of milk, cold lunch served in metal lunch box, bottled cider and a hard-boiled egg, a corncob, or a boiled potato—intensify the gulf between the predators and their prey. Although an even portion is given to every person in the spirit of fairness parading as equality, the stronger steal from the weak, making them even stronger. Deok-su and his gang form a clique to consolidate their power by means of intimidation and bullying. When Mi-nyeo attempts to benefit from alpha male Doek-su but soon falls out of favor, she immediately scouts Sang-woo, whom she sees as the next patron.

Mi-nyeo: Hey handsome *oppa*, who is the boss here? Are you the boss?

Sang-woo: We don't have such a thing here in this group.

Mi-nyeo: Oh, that's better. An equal society!

Mi-nyeo here ostensibly mocks the emphasis on the rules of equality heard in the guard's repeated announcements throughout the games. It is no wonder that she is the character who comes to denounce those rules, and the order of the dominant types at the top of the food chain soon reveals its limits: no matter how weak or strong the contestants, what creates real strength to defy the rule by iron fist is trust among team members, even in the games like tug-of-war, which ostensibly reward the physically strong. Gi-hun's seemingly weak team—with members including elderly Il-nam, three scrawny women, and a disabled foreign worker—end up overcoming their all-male opponents with their close collaboration.

Conversely, the physically strong team weakens with disintegrating teamwork and growing mistrust of one another. Think of the horrifying slaughterhouse scene where lawless violence explodes, with players killing one another for no obvious reasons. Where is the fairness of the rules? Where is equality for all? The only way to survive in this dog-eat-dog pandemonium is to stick together. Ali, Sae-byeok, Gi-hun, Sang-woo, and Il-nam watch each other's backs and endure the bloodbath—a necessary rehearsal for their tug-of-war teamwork. Sharing meals and giving up their meager food for others marks their temporary passage into an equal society. The reverse happens as well, when Gi-hun cleverly plants a seed of mistrust in Deok-su's head: "Do you trust your teammates? I wouldn't. Who do you think they will stab first when the lights go out tonight? It should be you, since you are the strongest." True to Gi-hun's provocation, Deok-su exits the game in the hands of Mi-nyeo, who evens the score with him when he betrays her. Mi-nyeo's vengeance brings fairness, if not equality. But at this solemn moment of final judgment for Deok-su, the thug divulges the most visceral truth of the games' fair rules before he falls off the bridge: "This is hell. There are no rules in hell."

FAKE REAL, REAL FAKE

The obsession with fairness and equality only reveals their lack in both concept and practice. The rules are restated over and over, but the overemphasis is nothing but an exposure of their absence. Even with the gruesome display of the violators' dead bodies, the touted fairness echoes as an empty rhetorical measure. Let's go back to the organ extraction room with the doctor-cum–Player 111 speaking in familiar terms with the guards. Unlike the hierarchical relationship akin to that of the jailor and the prisoner, in the operating room, the guards and the player speak freely to one another without using any honorifics. Even guards of various ranks speak without the strict barriers that usually separate them. But this patina of equality soon shatters into mistrust. Violence erupts and killing ensues. Without a foundational reliance upon one another, the performance of equality will remain merely that.

Returning to Il-nam reinforces this point. His weakness is most humiliatingly exposed when his incontinence is exposed. All the players perceive him to be the weakest contestant, but he is the only one who can make others live or die as he wishes. If the viewers read Il-nam's figure as an allegorical rendering of an aging population, then the seniors come back with full vengeance at the end. During the marble game, young players condescendingly refer to the game as "played by boomers." Well, youngsters, welcome to the world run by boomers, who can totally fool you or doom you to death.

Things are not what they appear to be—or what they claim to be—in the world of games. From fake equality to fake sky, confusion ensues as people are unable to tell what is real. When Il-nam goes to the arena for the marble game, he marvels at how realistic the set looks, even claiming that once upon a time, he lived in a house like this with his wife and son. Even death can be faked. The first player gunned down in red light, green light is at first perceived as faking death by the surrounding players. The reverse holds true as well in this confusing world: Gi-hun, in the final episode, is beyond shocked to discover that Il-nam did not die in the marble game. Existential crisis emerges in this world of counterfeits, and this is perhaps why the game participants are so invested in identifying themselves with their names and places of origin—to cling to any sense of authenticity.

On an island where their sole identity marker is the numbered tag by which they are referred to, the participants naturally cling to their given names as vestiges of ordinary social life. The more than 6 million individuals who lost their lives to COVID—with unique life trajectories and stories—would similarly resist being remembered simply as statistical data. Every time Gi-hun is given an opportunity, he introduces himself: "I am Gi-hun, Gi-hun from Ssangmundong." Gi-hun also names Sang-woo "the pride of Ssangmundong," as if it is some kind of hereditary title that ties the individual to their place of origin. After Mi-nyeo and Deok-su have a tryst in the bathroom, they exchange names as a sign of intimacy. During the marble game, Ji-yeong and Sae-byok exchange names as a marker of friendship before bidding each other a final farewell. After the tug-of-war, Mi-nyeo asks her teammates to call her by her first name. After Ali, Sang-woo, Gi-hun, and Sae-byeok stick together during the night of massacre, they exchange names as a sign of emotional closeness. It only makes sense that Il-nam pretends to have a hard time remembering his own name, since he has no reason to remind everyone—and himself—of his true identity. Likewise, Ji-yeong initially refuses to share her last name, because she joined the games with a wish to die.

But even the extraordinary emphasis on personal names might not always lead to truthful identification. The inordinate degree of emphasis comes from Mi-nyeo, literally meaning "beauty" in Korean, which is highly unlikely to be her real name. When she drops a lighter to help Deok-su during the honeycomb game, careful viewers are able to discern what's written on it: "Mi-nyeo's Lounge." Just like a stage name, it is most likely an adopted name for her intimate clients to use. As if turning our attention to the falsity of this identity marker, we hear in passing one of Deok-su's entourage giggle and note that the meaning of the name is lost on her. The uncertainty of existence is once again reified by Mi-nyeo herself when she begs the guards to release her after the red light, green light game, pleading that she just gave birth to a baby she did not have time to name and hence could not even register for a proper birth certificate. In the world filled with fakery, everyone clings to any faint signs of self-identification, which themselves could be destabilizing falsehoods. Would anyone be truly surprised if Mi-nyeo is fabricating a story about a nameless baby she never had?

The crisis of this drama may stem from how it is nearly impossible to tell real from fake and fake from real. The anxiety about disinformation to which we have been subject since even before the advent of COVID has changed the contours of everyday life, from the larger-scale presidential election results and disinformation campaign against COVID vaccination to the minutiae of daily interactions. We constantly doubt the veracity of any information we encounter: Is everything for real, or faking real? Amid the compounded confusion between reality and illusion, truth and its obfuscation, we are lost, especially in the face of emergent technologies such as deepfakes. With ever more sophisticated methods of fakery evolving, our judgment will become more and more dull.

The accelerated shift in media formats and technology is a pronounced symptom of the COVID era. The digital leap forward, just like the increasing wealth gap, deepened the divide between those with and those without. The concern for economic precarity and the wealth gap is also about digital access, since those with access and literacy not only survived but thrived under the pandemic, which has brought about the shifting hierarchy in media relations.

The impact of traditional TV shows has declined with the growing popularity of individual YouTubers, social media influencers, and the mind-boggling success of a few internet-based shows. YouTube channel programs such as *Try Guys* and *MrBeast*, both of which feature challenges involving trying something new via a gaming format—in the case of *MrBeast*, for a large cash prize—work on a premise akin to that of *Squid Game*. It is not surprising that this Korean-language Netflix show had no difficulty communicating to a global audience, since the rules were already well integrated into these wildly popular internet-based shows.

In a way, *Squid Game* is allegorically telling us that this is the new pattern of media consumption in the pandemic era, where consumers really have no decisions to make. Those who have the technology to do so will produce—even fabricate—truth, while depriving viewers of any critical means to discern what is real or not. Tongue in cheek, *Squid Game*, as the biggest beneficiary of the streaming consumption under the pandemic, is covertly reminding us that we really have no choice. If you ever think you do, watch out—it may be a fake one.

Without equality, fairness, and trustworthy information, do we really have a genuine freedom? Do the game players really have a choice between life and death? What kind of choice is it between losing your organs to loan sharks or dying on an island?

To flip a red folded disk or blue folded disk?

To press the red button or the green button?

To choose a star-shaped honeycomb or an umbrella-shaped honeycomb?

No matter which you choose, the game goes on. Just remember to play at your own risk.

3

PAINT YOUR DREAMS WITH BLOOD

A thirty-foot-tall animatronic five-year-old girl turns her head and covers her eyes. "Green light," she says (see figure on the following page). Surrounded by walls painted like the sky, 456 players, all in deep financial debt, take a step forward. "It was the most difficult and scary thing to film. It was like seeing 456 characters all move according to choreography, like watching a K-pop band, because all these people had to move and stop in unison. Should I be sad? Should I be shocked? Is this beautiful? Is this funny? I wanted the audience to feel confused visually," said Hwang on *Good Morning America*,[1] revealing the show's key ingredient: staging violent horror within sets and settings of childhood innocence. A moment later, the massive girl, in

The robot is inspired by a schoolgirl character, Young-hee, who appears in Korean elementary school textbooks.
MOVIESTORE COLLECTION / ALAMY STOCK PHOTO

pigtails and a cheery orange sundress, says, "Red light." As birds fly over fake wheat fields stretching in all directions, one participant is still moving. A gunshot sounds. His body falls. Another participant sees him coughing blood and runs. He's shot in the back, his blood splattering on a woman's face. She screams. She's shot in the head. Chaos ensues. But a few moments later, the girl reminds everyone that we're still playing. "Green light," she says, and the game goes on.

The previous chapter referred to *Squid Game* as a pungent social commentary on the precarious lives of economically disenfranchised subjects living the realities of the pandemic era. But let's not forget that much of the show's storytelling energy also comes from its sharp design elements. Villains with machine guns wear hot pink hoodies and commute to work on adorable pastel staircases. The participants sleep on cartoonishly high stacks of army barrack bunk beds. The walls, business cards, and game elements of this quasi prison rely on basic shapes like squares, circles, and triangles. These cacophonous combinations blur the lines between kindergarten classroom and a hyperreal slaughterhouse, inciting a bodily dissonance in viewers that lies beyond language, so is anyone truly surprised that *Squid Game* has managed to captivate global audiences despite its language barriers?

Let's start with the stairs. Our contestants and their hooded guards ascend and descend a spiral labyrinth in measured steps. Like a trail of ants marching to their queen, their movements become part of the visual play. The contestants, in their identical pine green tracksuits, match the stairs, bursting with bubblegum pink, chartreuse, and turquoise. But maybe they also merge with them. When walking the stairs, often on the way to their deaths or on their way back to their beds after barely surviving, the stairs reduce the contestants to just another design element. Just as social media creates a buzzing platform that's nothing without ants to bring it to life, the stairs make the contestants more vibrant while simultaneously treating them as replaceable cogs (see figure below).

Blinding the game contestants with jolly colors, the stairs induce a tonal vertigo for both the climbers and the viewer. Where the hell are we going? Why do we need to go in all these loop de loops to get there? In the capitalist world where function and use value reign supreme, why build a super confusing bubblegum staircase? The colors distract and distort, and the contestants forget what's real, forget the stakes. Such design is normally reserved

The colorful staircase design, inspired by Escher's various lithographs, is a tissue connecting contestants to various spatial settings on the island. MOVIESTORE COLLECTION / ALAMY STOCK PHOTO

for playgrounds and amusement parks, settings that toy with death but always bring you home safe at the end of the day. Yet in this case, they're actually marching players toward their own demise. The stairs reinforce what those in power prefer us to think: no matter how high the stakes, this is all a game.

Technically, the stairs are functional. They lead to various compartmentalized spaces featured throughout *Squid Game*: from the contestants' warehouse-like dormitory to the pink guards' isolated cells, from open gaming arenas to private control stations, from the Front Man's hideout to the basement crematorium. As the body count rises, the stairs remind us that all these elements coexist and feed off each other. The first episode is a prelude to how the director will keep on deploying the grotesque divide between indoor and outdoor settings to heighten the show's atmospheric tension. Contestants of the games are smuggled to an island to entertain the rich, but it is not a typical fantasy island adorned with sweeping panoramic views of emerald shores and coral reefs. Yet the interior grounds for the deadly games mimic nature. For red light, green light, wheat seems to extend in all directions. In the second game, the walls contain cartoonish clouds, puffs painted with a single line, as if by a kindergartener. Contrast that with blinding florescent lighting of the gymnasium-style room with the bunk bed stacks. With the stark juxtaposition between fake beauty and harsh realism, viewers may think of directors such as Stanley Kubrick or David Lynch. Beauty often coexists with the ominous. Beauty often conceals a trap.

Squid Game uses the stairs to generate that foreboding mood. We might call the set design of the show a "House of Stairs," inspired by the Dutch graphic artist M. C. Escher's famous lithograph *Relativity* featuring an intricate staircase (see figure on the following page). Art director Chae Kyoung-sun noted that she had always wanted to create a set that paid open homage to Escher's famous stairs.[2] But *Squid Game* was by no means the first popular film to visually cite Escher. Films such as *Labyrinth* (1986) and *Inception* (2010) and the family-friendly show *The Simpsons* have all honored Escher, playing with relativity and interconnectedness of objects inhabiting the same space. Escher himself commented on how *Relativity* reveals how certain objects can trip up the field of vision when a single gravitational force becomes multiplied into several dimensions: "In this picture, three gravitational forces operate perpendicularly to one another. We are walking in crisscrosses on the floor and stairs. Some of them, though belonging to different worlds, come very close together

M. C. Escher's "Relativity" (1953) has served as inspiration for many films and dramas, including *Squid Game*. © 2022

but can't be aware of one another's existence."[3] By detaching from spatial logic and making multiple planes exist at once, Escher's stairs confuse reality and illusion, two-dimensionality and three-dimensionality.

While Hwang singled out *Relativity* as a primary source of inspiration, it is perhaps Escher's *Convex and Concave* (see figure on the following page) that resonates more closely

Of many lithographs of staircases produced by M. C. Escher, "Convex and Concave" (1955) most closely reflect the rules of the world in *Squid Game*. © 2022 THE M.C. ESCHER COMPANY-THE NETHERLANDS. ALL RIGHTS RESERVED. WWW.MCESCHER.COM

with the idea behind the stair design in *Squid Game*. Created in 1955, Escher's lithographic print further explored how one element may represent two oppositional shapes and how seemingly opposite elements become entangled into a single shape. Escher himself emphasized the piece's ability to disclose hidden logics of connectivity: "Things are uncertain and can be seen in two different ways: a floor is also a ceiling; an interior is also an exterior; concave is at the same time a convex."[4] The reversible nature of two contradictory elements feels essential to *Squid Game*, eliminating any certainty about wrong and right, child and adult, rich and poor. A nod to Escher's work endows the staircase design with the gravitational forces of unknowability where the instantaneous reversal of fate becomes entirely possible.

The illusion of social mobility travels up and down the pastel staircase in *Squid Game*, where even the most daring traveler is bound to get lost. Chae revealed in an interview that the original design of the gaming arena included a sectional elevation of staircases meant to elucidate how each floor is connected to another. But the conventional architectural plan was soon abandoned to clear a passage for chaos and confusion to emerge. So entangled were the staircases that even the director and actors literally got lost while navigating the maze.[5] No surprise that the infamous stairs are often compared to Bong Joon-ho's *Parasite*, a cinematic masterpiece that captured the visceral divide between the wealthy and the poor inscribed onto the cityscape of Seoul itself. Bong's stairs are neither a conspicuous homage to Escher nor an artificially built set. What connects the directors' vision is how they find both joy and terror in the vertigo-inducing height (see figures on the following page). Bong told Hwang several times how much he "loves vertical space";[6] Hwang's *Squid Game* is a

Bong Joon-ho's *Parasite* features several steep staircases that actually exist in Seoul. This one was featured during the rainy night when Gi-woo's family had to make a sudden escape from the hilltop mansion of their employee. UPI / ALAMY STOCK PHOTO

The entrance to Gi-woo's semibasement house also features precipitous stairs. NIPPON NEWS / ALAMY STOCK PHOTO

nod to Bong's proclivity, where confused steps could easily lead anyone to a reversal of fortune.

In the topsy-turvy world of *Squid Game*, the same principle could apply to the hot pink uniforms of the guards, which may first appear consistent with the deceptively jovial color palette of the show. But the hot pink color, often associated with the vibrant, youthful femme products, now conceals the guards' darkness, the naked bloodiness of their greed and inhumanity, dripping with the pain of the players they nonchalantly massacre (see figure below). In almost any other military or police-adjacent uniform, the color serves to camouflage but also embolden

The pink guards' ranks are marked by the geometric shapes on their masks. The guards with triangular masks are middle-step guards. ENTERTAINMENT PICTURES / ALAMY STOCK PHOTO

the plebes inside the clothes. As pop artist Patty Gone asks, "How would American police officers react if they had to wear hot pink every day? The color both emasculates the guards of *Squid Game* while also making their actions appear more cartoonishly harsh, as if they were Teletubbies with machine guns, or gay Stormtroopers at the gym."[7]

The only non-pink element of the guards' wardrobe is their masks, rounded black shells demarcated with white geometric shapes (see figure below). The imprints of circles, triangles, and squares reveal their hierarchy: circles for the lowest-ranking unarmed workers, triangles for the armed middlemen, and square for the highest-ranking managers.

Circles on pink guards' masks denote their entry level.
ENTERTAINMENT PICTURES / ALAMY STOCK PHOTO

The art director revealed in an interview that "angularity equates power in *Squid Game*'s geometric design."[8] More lines equal more power. Marking the highest rank among guards, the square's equal number of edges and vertices by no means symbolizes social equality. Careful viewers of the show might have noticed in episode 1 that the logo of Daehan Bank, shown at a moment when Gi-hun tries to withdraw cash with his mother's ATM card, features variations of the square shape. Inherent within money, the square, the bill, the paper cash with corners, hides the illusion that anyone can get it, if they play the game properly. But we all know the system is fixed. Those who have the squares make the rules.

Stuck between lower-ranking circles and higher-ranking squares, triangles capture the desire for upward mobility. Looming large behind the shape of triangle is the primal urge to step on the shoulders of the weak to occupy the top vertex. The pyramid shape has long been associated with lopsided power: from hundreds of enslaved people building monumental triangular tombs for Egyptian Pharaohs to the stage design for the Korean idol survival show *Produce 101*. A popular reality show produced by the Korean media conglomerate CJ ENM from 2016 to 2019, *Produce 101* featured one hundred one hopefuls training and competing against one another to be anointed as pop

In CJ ENM's idol recruitment reality show *Produce 101*, the pyramid shape marks the passage of competition and survival that would-be idols have to take. BY MNET / WIKIMEDIA COMMONS

stars by CJ ENM's management. A triangle makes up the show's logo (see figure above), a design choice mirrored by the show's stage set, which arranged the contestants in a massive pyramid. Similar to *Squid Game, Produce 101's* contestants all wear the same uniform, crashed together in the dormitory, and were surveilled at all times. Each episode culminates with the host proclaiming that night's winner, leading to a full-blown coronation ceremony with the winner ascending to the top of the triangle. But the triangle can just as easily invert. The following week, the crowned winner often tumbles down the power structure. This constant movement entertains audience members by providing the illusion that social climbing is possible for themselves, while giving them the satisfaction of voting against those on top of the pyramid and tearing them down. The triangle's ups and downs reinforce the idea of society as an inevitably cutthroat game of climbing and falling, winning and losing, in an infinite loop.

At the bottom of the geometric hierarchy lies that loop, the circle. The design logic of *Squid Game* proposes that curves sit far from the hard edges of power. In episode 3, the character Gi-hun must choose between four shapes for that day's game, and he picks the curved umbrella, mostly because it reminds him of the last time he saw his daughter, standing in the rain during episode 2. But making choices based on emotional attachments don't work out for him—the umbrella is the most difficult shape of the four to extricate from its casing, and he almost loses. If we take the curves a step further, they may call to mind the slippery organs of the game's dead victims lifted out of their lifeless bodies. Though we're made of vulnerabilities, of circles and curves, the game ensures we conceal them.

On the eve of the games' finale, the three remaining contestants—Gi-hun, Sang-woo, and Sea-byeok—eat an exquisite banquet before entering their final game. Seated on the three sides of a huge triangular banquet table, they each look into the eyes of their two opponents as guards serve them an opulent steak dinner. Their gazes, and the camera's close-ups on those gazes, mediate the power balance among themselves, each contestant vying for a way to the top of the triangle.

Yet an aerial view of the banquet brings all three key geometric shapes into a convergence. The triangular table rests upon a floor of tiny squares, nodding to checker and chess boards, with the whole arrangement framed in a circle (see figure below). The circles, squares, and triangles acquire such significance through their relationships with one another. Just like in Escher's *Convex and Concave*, elements mix until

The last banquet hosted for the three remaining contestants features all three shapes found on the masks of the guards—circle, square, and triangle—in a dimly lit interior space reminiscent of the haunting symmetrical designs in David Lynch's *Twin Peaks* or Alejandro Jodorowsky's *Holy Mountain.* AUTHOR'S COLLECTION

the ground feels unstable. Though squares may allude to the highest-ranking guards, the triangle, the struggle for power, remains central. The three players, artificially garbed as professional players in their theatrical tuxedos, appear as knights on a grand chessboard that can only be fully captured by the all-surveilling eye. These survivors' placement as chess knights harks all the way back to Gi-hun's fascination with horse racing, but more immediately, to the previous stepping-stone game, where bridge crossers were represented by crystal horses—to be advanced or knocked off the bridge. On this round game board, which horse will get knocked off next (see figure below)?

The spectral emptiness that separates individual diners from one another is haunted by the countless dead players

The dormitory for contestants, once overcrowed by 456 players, is now empty. But the vacuous space appears to be haunted by those who once inhabited it. NETFLIX

who once occupied that same space with the finalists. As they devour their bloody rare steaks and garnet-colored wine, they look like the predators they've become. They've made it this far on the blood of others. And one of them, Sae-byeok, is literally bleeding to death from the deep abdomen wound she received in the previous game, blood spilling as she consumes blood (see figure below). The candlelit symmetric feast and grandiose dreamlike scale nods to the Black Lodge in David Lynch's *Twin Peaks* (1992) or the temple in Alejandro Jodorowsky's *Holy Mountain* (1973), seeming more grotesque due to their impeccably designed settings.

Sae-byeok hides her fatal abdominal injury in order to survive the final passage to winning. MOVIE STORE COLLECTION / ALAMY STOCK PHOTO

Yet, far before this banquet scene, *Squid Game* employs gargantuan sets and props, starting with the oversized Yeong-hee robot, modeled after a familiar girl figure from a Korean elementary school textbook, to the multistory bunk beds that dwarf the contestants. But one of the most surprising may be the mammoth playground of the second game. A slide, a jungle gym, and a merry-go-round, each at least five stories tall, all blazing in bright primary colors, greet the contestants, as if placing pressure on players to enjoy themselves (see figure below). While the artificial sky on the walls during the first game created the illusion

A perspective from the top of the gargantuan slide dwarfs the players and the guards alike. Massive-scale play structures induce fear in game participants, but they also make guards look like ants. ALBUM / ALAMY STOCK PHOTO

that the room was a vast wheatfield, the second game's setting feels like a nursery, decorated by the toddler. Puffy single-line clouds tinted with soft powder blue nod to amatuerishness, not the outdoors (see figure below). In a world where failing to play children's games marks an invitation to irreversible death, cheerful décor reinstates the dark metaphor that the game doesn't get darker as you grow older. The game has always been dark.

If the first and the second games rely on disproportionately large props, then the third and the fifth games use altitude to induce fear. Both tug-of-war and stepping-stone share design elements and were actually constructed.

The unlikely combination of guns and childish design produces grotesque effects. ALBUM / ALAMY STOCK PHOTO

Though it would have been easy to shoot with a green screen, the set designers built these death-defying elevated platforms balanced on poles.

The set for tug-of-war looks like a construction site–cum-guillotine. Its cargo elevators and an extensive use of yellow, alluding to caution tape, evokes the idea that perpetuates itself: the greed machine must be perpetually under construction (see figure below). The stepping-stone set, on the other hand, goes full theatrical. When the sixteen players enter the arena, it's as if they were pushed onto a proscenium stage without knowing their lines. Circus-like string lights reveal the contours of the fragile walkway made of tempered glass designed to sustain their body weight and

The scene features an agoraphobic design of a disconnected bridge where the losing team must fall and die in the "Tug of War" game. NETFLIX

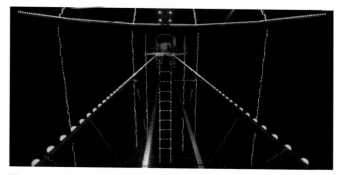

The set for the "Stepping Stone" game presents a hybrid design that mixes elements of a circus marquee and a proscenium stage. NETFLIX

normal glass that will shatter, leading to death at the bottom of the pit (see figure above).

Circus performers risk falls, injuries, and occasional death, but in the stepping-stone game there is no upward flight, no trapeze artists or tumbling acrobats, only the potential to fall into the abyss. Though the fallen bodies lying in the dark abyss below are only partially visible, they make the circus scenario all the more terrifying (see figure on the following page). The only way to win is by standing over the dead bodies of those who walked before you, to literally feel their weight. No matter the game, the winners walk on the losers' backs, and the winners have to deal with that guilt. When Gi-hun returns home with his prize money, he finds his mother in her basement room,

The fear-filled faces of the "Stepping Stone" contestants betray the jolly design of the set. ENTERTAINMENT PICTURES / ALAMY STOCK PHOTOS

lying motionless in the dark. Her barely discernable dead face harkens back to the closeness of death during the stepping-stone game. Could Gi-hun's mother have passed away when he was crossing the bridge of life and death?

Squid Game masters the psychology of fear with its careful use of lighting throughout all nine episodes. The most horrific sequence arrives in episode 4. The organizers of the game design a scheme to eliminate weak contestants before commencing the fourth game. By supplying only one hard-boiled egg and a bottle of soda to the physically and emotionally exhausted contestants, the guards effectively set up a hostile environment between the players, breaking the players into factions. Then, to everyone's horror, Deok-su kills a man over a bottle of soda. But instead of facing consequences, he's indirectly rewarded: the players watch as prize money reserved for Deok-su's victim drops into the glowing piggy bank suspended from the ceiling. The system replaces a life with money right before their eyes.

As abhorrent as this incident might have been, it is just a precursor to the main killing spree to follow that night. Having learned of the immunity given to lawless predators, gangs congeal around Deok-su and start a deadly fight once the lights go out. The gang attacks anyone in their way, and carnage wrecks the dormitories. And instead of using his power to squelch the chaos, the Front Man flickers the florescent lights, amplifying the slaughter by allowing the fighters to see their prey, and the nausea-inducing rapid alternation between darkness and light leads to mistaken identity. Who's killing who, and why, becomes a blur.

Squid Game often employs strobing florescent light to heighten confusion. The dormitory-turned–slaughter house scene in episode 4 harkens back to episode 2 when the police officer Hwang Jun-ho enters the dilapidated room of his brother. While investigating his elder brother's disappearance after receiving a mysterious invitation card to participate in the game, Jun-ho enters his brother's room with hopes of understanding his absent sibling.

Although much smaller in scale and impact than the killing spree sequence in the episode "Stick to the Team," the light flickers for a few seconds when Jun-ho turns on the switch, as the camera spies a René Magritte book on the desk, panning to show a painting by the Belgian surrealist hanging in the window. Depicting a strange juxtaposition of the luminous sky with the nocturnal street, this 1954 piece by Magritte is perhaps the best-known work in his *Empire of Light* series, a collection of paintings central to the trajectory of surrealism that the artist produced from the 1940s to 1960s.

Surreal, disorienting lighting inspired the film poster of the horror classic *The Exorcist* (1973), while also being whimsical, prodding viewers to ponder the contradictory synchronicity of diurnal and nocturnal time zones (see figure on the following page). Magritte himself championed the painting's ability to expose ideas that are not rational within the logics of the vision alone:

> The conception of a picture, that is, the idea, is not visible in the picture: an idea cannot be seen with the eyes. What is represented in a picture is what is visible to the eyes, it is the thing or things that must have been ideated. Thus, what

Rene Magritte's 1954 painting in the series *The Empire of Light*.
PEGGY GUGGENHEIM COLLECTION, VENICE (SOLOMON R. GUGENHEIM
FOUNDATION, NEW YORK)

are represented in the picture *The Empire of Light* are the things I ideated, i.e., a nighttime landscape and a sky such as we see during the day. The landscape evokes night and the sky evokes day. I call this power: poetry.[9]

According to Magritte, the painting unveils the limits of practical vision. He painted what lies beyond the visible by opening up the powerful eyes of the mind to read ideas and imaginations, similar to how Escher's concave and convex alter conventional perspectives. *Squid Game* introduces the 1954 version of *The Empire of Light* at a moment when mystery and suspense reach an inflection point. Jun-ho steps into the enigmatic world of his missing brother, who had altruistically given him one of his kidneys. Nonetheless, by the end of the show, the act of brotherly love is toppled by the harrowing discovery that the missing brother is the Front Man, the chief executor of the deadly games. The world of games closely mimics the sharp chiaroscuro of the *The Empire of Light* itself, where contradictory truths coexist.

Magritte's chiaroscuro defines the luminosity of the island. At the end of episode 1, viewers see an aerial view of the island under the bright sunlight. We see the large outdoor arena of red light, green light from above, an indoor space with an automatic sliding roof. Obstructing the sunlight bifurcates the island into sunny sky and dark interior, just like *The Empire of Light*. The island's subterranean area where guards incinerate dead bodies, a cavelike crematorium, is bathed in black and inspired by an ant colony swarming with worker ants in their coordinated marches. Just like their crawling counterparts, the faceless pink guards align hundreds of coffins like seasoned factory workers. The scene turns even more preposterous when we realize that the dark coffins take the shape of gift boxes wrapped in pretty pink ribbons. Why place the brutally murdered corpses in gift boxes (see figure below)?

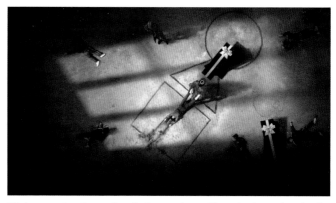

Pink guards place dead players in coffins designed to look like gift boxes. ENTERTAINMENT PICTURES / ALAMY STOCK PHOTO

Gorgeous pink ribbons on charcoal-colored coffins may come across as a scathing mockery of death, but this design choice presents a carefully planned maneuver to expose the central vision of the show: that according to the rules of *Squid Game*, life and death are hardly discernable modes of existence. Even more, death might be the best gift for those who live their lives in a state of morbid despair.

Squid Game ties death's grimness and the celebration of life together when cash-strapped Gi-hun goes to an arcade to win a birthday present for his daughter in episode 1. With no money to buy even a small present, he desperately tries his luck with a claw machine. After several failed attempts, Gi-hun manages to fish a small black gift box out of a heap of cheaply made stuffed animals. Not knowing the contents of the box, Gi-hun nonetheless presents it to his daughter, who excitedly opens it, only to be disappointed by a black toy gun arranged on hot pink wrapping paper. An obvious nod to the guards' costumes, this scene forecasts the morbid events to follow. Later, Jun-ho finds his missing brother's invitation to the games inside a box, also pink and black. The passage from trivial to fatal hinges upon the consistent use of this color palette, the simultaneity of a color that celebrates a child's birth with the color of guns and violence. Yet the most ingenious design element of this circle of life and death may be the gift exchange throughout *Squid Game*. To understand the layered meaning behind the gift box design, let's consider the show's twisted philosophy on the practice of gift giving.

Early twentieth-century anthropologists Marcel Mauss, Bronislaw Malinowski, and their intellectual descendants explored the practice of gift giving in non-Western societies as a way to understand various forms of economic exchange that preceded the advent of the monetary system. These scholars assumed that before currency was in place, a barter system governed primitive societies, but when taking a closer look, these barters were gifts. The practice of mutual gift giving in endless spirals and on all sorts of scales bound these societies together. Gift giving was a reciprocal act that greased social relationships, and as such, gifts received were not to be accumulated but given away. To this point, British social anthropologist Wendy James notes that among the Uduk in northeast Africa, "any wealth transferred from one subclan to another, whether animals, grain or money, is in the nature of gift, and should be consumed, and not invested for growth. If such transferred wealth is added to the subclan's capital [cattle, in this case] and kept for growth and investment, the subclan is regarded as being in an immoral relation of debt to the donors of the original gift."[10]

Jacques Derrida would disagree. According to Derrida, if the gift giver receives gratitude, it contaminates the nature of gift. Gift giving is an unadulterated act of pure sacrifice, the pinnacle of which comes in the form of death.[11] The purest gift is the one you give and die, foreclosing any possibility of a reciprocal act from the recipient. For example, Lewis Hyde notes that the gift giver's choice of gift is irrelevant of the recipient's intentionality: "A gift is a thing we do not get by our own efforts. We cannot buy it; we cannot acquire it through an act of will. It is bestowed upon us."[12] A gift is given, not exchanged.

In between these two poles lies a theological view as championed by John Milbank, who notes that a gift may take the form of religious sacrifice given in the form of self-obliteration. But while such unrooted love is not impossible, what makes a gift a gift is human mutuality, dependency, and reciprocity. And because human mutuality depends on gift giving and exchange, the idea of the beneficiary is already embedded in the notion of gift. Gifts are predicated by the presence of someone who anticipates love and expresses gratitude. For Milbank, there has to be anticipated gratitude and love from the recipient for the gift to be recognized as a gift. In short, the gift is interpersonal, mutually dependent, and reciprocal.[13]

The gifts in *Squid Game* neither exalt nor completely denounce these ideas. This ambiguity may leave viewers dazzled and confused. The gifts of life and death bring no ultimate release. For those contestants who give up their lives for the games, is death freedom or their gift to their fellow contestants? And for the final winner, is the prize money a gift or a curse?

Squid Game toys with gifts, starting with its askew representation of the barter system. In the very first episode, a man in a well-tailored suit and leather briefcase approaches the forlorn Gi-hun as he waits for a homebound train. The mysterious man proposes a game of *ddakji*—or flipping folded paper disks—betting 100,000 won each time. When penniless Gi-hum loses and cannot pay the mysterious man, the latter responds with a seductive proposal: "If you don't have money, pay back with your body." With no other available options, Gi-hun pays the debt by offering his cheek for a vicious slap across the face. But when the mysterious man loses, instead of getting slapped, he hands Gi-hun crisp paper bills with an elegant smile. This is not two equals making a barter; what is being exchanged is the bodily pain of those who have nothing else to give and the luxury of avoiding pain by those who have the means.

Barter continues to reveal the true faces of key players. When Ali is given a breakfast bread by Sang-woo, he remembers it and makes sure he saves his potato to return Sang-woo's favor. But Ali's voluntary gift giving—or more precisely, gift returning—is met only by Sang-woo's blunt gift demanding. Cornered by proximity to death when he is down to just one marble in episode 6, Sang-woo kneels down and begs Ali to save him by giving up the marbles. Soon his pleading voice turns into a more forceful demand: Ali came this far thanks to his savvy gaming tactics. In complete desperation, Sang-woo falls so low as to remind Ali of the small bus fee he gave him when they were temporarily released, in return asking Ali to give up his own life.

This disproportionate barter soon spirals into degenerate gift giving. At the final meal, an automated announcement welcomes the three finalists: "Tonight's banquet is a gift to express our thanks to the finalists who have shown dedication to the games. This is a token of our hope that you will show even better fighting spirit in the final game. Please enjoy your dinner without any worries." The gift of the banquet is conditional, a two-way exchange in which the Front Man and VIPs expect to be paid back with brutal entertainment. The perverse nature of this supposedly gracious announcement climaxes when the guards-cum-waiters clear the empty plates and utensils but leave a sharp steak knife in front of each player to be used by the players-cum-diners on each other.

However, occasionally *Squid Game* digresses, introducing the purist notion of gift giving without any expectations for reciprocity. In episode 6, a pair of players compete in a ten-minute marble game to determine who lives and who dies. Sea-byeok partners with Ji-yeong, a fragile girl of a similar age, and when the girls learn the elimination rules, they decide not to waste time on the game but to candidly disclose their life stories instead (see figure on the following page). While the others play a desperate game with their lives on the line, the girls talk and listen. Ji-yeong confesses that she killed her sexually predatory father. Sae-byeok recalls losing her family members to an epidemic in North Korea. Their stories act as a prelude to Ji-yeong's unconditional sacrifice for Sae-byeok: she intentionally loses and dies so her friend can live.

The harrowing game of life and death unfolds on a set that faithfully re-creates the cradle of childhood, where friendship and enmity were forged around playing

Ji-yeong and Sae-byeok pair up for deadly marble games, but instead of wasting their time on deciding who gets to live and who gets to die, they share their inner secrets in raw honesty. The friendship between the two players emerges in a striking set inspired by Kim Ki-chan's photography. NETFLIX

harmless games. Chae revealed in an interview that the design for this sixth episode was "inspired by the documentary photography of Kim Ki-chan," whose oeuvre presents an intimate perspective on the bygone era.[14] Kim's photography is akin to a time machine that enables contemporary viewers to enter a heartwarming memory lane with humor and compassion and encounter what we have lost as a result of rapid urban development. The texture of broken bricks, hastily erected electric poles, and thin metal roofs all come to life in these photographs (see figures on the following two pages). Even under the shade of skyscrapers and highways, weeds and moss sprout through

Photo taken in May 1976 in Jungrim-dong, Seoul.
PHOTO BY KIM KI-CHAN

the cracks of concrete walls and pavement as they become illuminated by the bright faces of the back-alley dwellers.

But *Squid Game* spills a coat of blood onto Kim's black-and-white world of innocence—not just through the tonal terror of the blazing sky but also by destroying every child that lives in an adult. The show counters Ji-yeong's voluntary death with chilling parody. In the same episode, during Gi-hun and Il-nam's marble match, Il-nam gives Gi-hun his last marble, his last bid for life, as a nod to their status as *gganbu*, friends who share everything. Faced with the harrowing prospect of death, Gi-hun accepts the gift and sheds tears as he walks away, Il-nam dead. This heart-wrenching moment, which moved many viewers to tears, is later

Photo taken in June 1982 in Jungrim-dong, Seoul.

upended when Il-nam emerges at the end of the series mysteriously unharmed. To Gi-hun's shock, this frail old man was the mastermind behind the games who toyed with Gi-hun out of boredom. What initially appeared to be an act of selfless sacrifice turns out to be a bargaining chip for exchange where Il-nam, while pretending to suffer from dementia, reaps the pleasure of manipulating desperate Gi-hun. Il-nam's deception turns the act of unconditional gift giving into a theatrical gimmick, cheapening the seemingly altruistic sacrifice. The cruelty of Il-nam's act is made ever more clear by how Ji-yeong's unconditional gift giving to her game partner ("Shall we bet everything on one marble?") is matched by Il-nam's enjoyment of his partner's suffering ("Shall we bet everything we have?").

Behind the nostalgic design of the back alleys and the pleasantness of gift boxes lurks the unnerving elimination of mutual human dependency. It therefore comes as no surprise that when Gi-hun visits his *gganbu* on his deathbed, Il-nam asks whether Gi-hun still trusts people. Il-nam's question is a naked confession of his inability to trust others, even on his deathbed. At this critical moment, still suffering from the joyless nature of life, Il-nam proposes another game to Gi-hun, and in exchange, promises to tell him why he devised the games. For the last game before death takes his last breath away, Il-nam points to a homeless man left alone on the frosty street. The heartless skeptic bets that no one will come to save the man, whereas Gi-hun, still believing in the kindness of strangers, takes the bet that a passerby will save the man before clock ticks midnight. Till the last moment, Il-nam sides with and reinforces the selfishness of humankind over mutual dependency and interpersonal support.

These conflicting perspectives on mankind, as illustrated in the last showdown between Il-nam and Gi-hun, builds as the nine episodes progress. In the last squid game, Sang-woo's self-centeredness and Gi-hun's feeling of indebtedness to other humans clash on the eve of the final match. Sang-woo's quest to win has turned dark. Well before he confronts Gi-hun, Sang-woo had already killed many. First, he deceives Ali during the marble game, leading to his death. Then he harshly criticizes Player 069 who's suffering from terrible guilt after losing his wife. Again, Sang-woo does not literally kill him, but his manipulation of Player 069 ("If you feel so guilty, why did you not die instead of your wife?") drives the man to suicide. Sang-woo's gradual development into villainous killer reaches a tipping point when he actually pushes a man with his own hands off the glass stepping-stones. Gi-hun is shocked and angered by Sang-woo, who kills the former glass factory worker who was hard at work trying to discern the tempered glass from the ordinary glass so the remaining players could cross the bridge safely.

Gi-hun: Why did you do it?

Sang-woo: What is your point?

Gi-hun: Why did you push that man?

Sang-woo: [scoffs] Why, did you start to feel quite generous, cause luck had you cross that bridge last? What if that man suddenly started acting like Deok-su, who refused to advance? Then what would you have done?

Gi-hun: He was on the last tile. He surely was planning to go.

Sang-woo: [raising his voice] How can you be so sure? He was a brute who knew how to discern different types of glasses, but he just stood in the back and let others fall and die.

Gi-hun: Whatever it is, you and I survived thanks to him.

Sang-woo: Bullshit. I don't know about you, but the reason I am still alive is not thanks to that guy. The reason I stand here alive is because I worked dead hard to survive.

Gi-hun: No matter what excuse you come up with, you are just a murderer of an innocent man.

Sang-woo: [shouting at the top of his lungs] Come back to your senses! If you want to walk away with that prize money, everyone else has to die.

Sang-woo erupts with brutal honesty (see figure below). In his mind, he got here on his own. Sang-woo's perspective resonates with that of Il-nam, who also sees the individual's self-advancing willpower as the key justification for enjoying enormous wealth. It is Il-nam who tells Gi-hun, "The prize money is the reward for your effort and the luck you

Sang-woo shows his true colors when confronted by Gi-hun.
ALBUM / ALAMY STOCK PHOTO

had. You have the right to spend it." Il-nam and Sang-woo both believe in the individual. Therefore, it's not shocking when Sang-woo pitilessly eliminates Sae-byeok in the last game before she even has a chance to play. Selfish fear, justified as strategy, guides him.

Gi-hun, on the other hand, feels the weight of the dead. Even in the last moments, he searches for ways to coexist with his opponents, first asking severely wounded Sae-byeok to form a team, and then refusing to kill Sang-woo so they can both walk away from the game's finale. As a character who clearly feels empathy for the other contestants, Gi-hun can't spend the prize money when he returns to the world. What makes *Squid Game* a powerful drama is not the sharp contrast between Gi-hun and Sang-woo, but their sticky entanglements, their symbiotic coexistence. Director Hwang noted in an interview that he envisioned Gi-hun and Sang-woo as twins. Like the two sides of the same coin, or like Escher's convex and concave (see figure on the following page). We all have Gi-hun and Sang-woo in us.

The twin image resurfaces when the Front Man gazes into a mirror and confronts his brother's stare. This haunting symmetry also plays out in the previous episode, when Jun-ho shoots the Front Man, not yet knowing his true identity. The Front Man then has no choice but to shoot

Gi-hun and Sang-woo, the two finalists of the game, show diametrically opposed personality traits, but they also complement each other as concave and convex.
AUTHOR'S COLLECTION

his brother back, and their bodily wounds mirror each other, two divergent paths from the same family.

So much of *Squid Game*'s storytelling technique relies on colors, shapes, and sounds that blur fear and amusement. In the end, the show's design is an allegorical question posed to all of us living in today's hypercompetitive world, which, unfortunately, resembles *Squid Game*. Can we collaborate and support each other? To extend the complementary nature of convex and concave to a broader scale, we see how the reverse-shot camera work presents the guards and the contestants as mutually entangled in the grid of desire and demise (see figures on the following page). Although the green and pink at first are separated chromatically, Chae

The scene captures the perspective of the guard looking down on contestants. ALBUM / ALAMY STOCK PHOTO

The camera adopts the perspective of the contestant, located on the top tier of the stacked-up bunkbeds looking down on the guards. MOVIESTORE COLLECTION / ALAMY STOCK PHOTO

made sure that "the pink guards sleep in the green rooms and then the contestants in green tracksuits travel along pink staircases."[15] They are more similar than different. Those surveilling are also surveilled. Those hunting are also hunted. We can never be mutually exclusive.

Once all the beds are cleared, we can easily see six familiar pictograms drawn on the dormitory walls. These images of red light, green light, honeycomb, tug-of-war, marble game, stepping-stone, and squid game could have given contestants early clues about the forthcoming games (see figure below). Had every contestant collaborated on discovering what common fate might await them, many more could have survived. Instead, most contestants took the games as cutthroat, winner-take-all games. They waited for

The pictograms on the wall foretell all six games that contestants are invited to play. NETFLIX

others to die, with the full reveal coming far too late. The writing on the wall was there all along.

In *Squid Game*, the rules claimed that those who passed all six games would win, meaning that, technically, everyone could have emerged a winner. It did not have to be a winner-take-all elimination game. The third rule of the game—that the games will stop if the majority of the players vote to opt out of the game—also ensured that the players could collectively decide to live together by letting go of their prize money. Instead of mutual support and generosity, they all walk as individuals into a meatgrinder that shaves 456 contestants to one. One could say the lack of human reciprocity killed them all, including the sole survivor of the game, Gi-hun, who, at the end of the show, feels like a dead man walking.

CODA

The Stakes of the Game

Long after the final game was over, the rabid heat lingered on in the arena. Even after *Squid Game* slid down the Netflix chart, giving the top position to newer sensations, the enthusiasm did not wane. Those fully addicted to the raw exasperation kept regurgitating bits and pieces of the show in an endless loop: from sharing the best honeycomb recipe to analyzing the zodiac-based interpersonal chemistries between the players and the viewers, from a psychoanalytic reading of the set design to a conspiracy theory in which a dead character is still alive, the internet hummed with *Squid Game* memes and retweets. A glass manufacturer based in Yorkshire, England, seized the opportunity to publish an article on how to tell tempered glass from ordinary glass, heavily promoting his company's products along the way.[1] High-profile YouTuber *MrBeast* certainly could not be left out of the buzz. Having poured $3.5 million (US) into re-creating the *Squid Game* experience, he easily recouped his investment with the enormous profit generated by this spinoff content. With this enterprise came the full closing of the circle—a drama, originally inspired by game shows, came back to inspire the creation of a new game show. Such a boomerang effect is typical of the transmedial connection for which Korean popular culture has become quite famous.

But even the seemingly infinite online domain was not big enough to contain the heat wave. It soon spilled out onto the streets and squares. With Halloween season on the horizon, the demand for *Squid Game*–inspired costumes exploded, bringing about a temporary economic boom for Seoul garment manufacturers (see top figure on the following page).

Whether Netflix-sanctioned official merchandise or unlicensed knockoffs, little figurines of pink guards and green contestants flooded display windows and pop-up stores in shopping malls around the globe (see bottom figure on the following page). Not to be satisfied with passive consumption, more participation-minded proponents of

The garment-manufacturing district in South Korea enjoyed a seasonal boom with the increased demand for *Squid Game*-themed Halloween costumes. KIM HONG-JI / ALAMY STOCK PHOTO

Squid Game-inspired merchandise filled a stand in a Southern California shopping mall. PHOTO BY MICHAEL BERRY

Following the enthusiastic reception of *Squid Game*,
a Young-hee doll made an appearance in major global
cities such as Sydney, Australia. RICHARD MILNES / ALAMY
STOCK PHOTO

the games took their fascination out in public. From Los
Angeles to Manila, Rotterdam to Sydney, it became common to see a large crowd playing red light, green light and
honeycomb in the fall of 2021 (see figure above).

The desire and demand to taste more turned to the production team itself. In interview after interview, Hwang,
who had barely had a chance to recover from directing
the first season, was asked about the next season. Even the
actors, while still shooting the first season, kept inquiring
about the possibility of a sequel.[2] The drama might have
critiqued the capitalist expansion of greed, but now the

show was creating a black hole that knew no satiation. No zealous response of such a degree goes unnoticed by the global internet TV network. Buoyed by the success of the first season, Netflix soon announced a second season to meet popular demand.[3] The instant gratification promised by Netflix founder Reed Hastings ("No more waiting. No more watching on a schedule that's not your own. No more frustration. Just Netflix") was about to be indulged in to the fullest.[4] But can worthy productions be cobbled together in an assembly line so rapidly? Let's not forget that Hwang had a decade to develop the first season of *Squid Game*.

Meanwhile, other "Made in Korea" dramas trailed the success of *Squid Game*, some more closely than others. Introduced roughly one month after the release of *Squid Game*, *My Name* streamed on Netflix on October 15, 2021, to much fanfare. Unlike the genre-bending *Squid Game*, *My Name* appeared to be a more conventional crime thriller spattered with gritty noir and visceral action sequences, landing in third place on the US Netflix chart. One K-drama that replicated the success more closely was *Hellbound*, topping the worldwide Netflix chart just one day after its release. Written and directed by Yeon Sang-ho, whose previous film credits include zombie classics such as

Train to Busan (2016) and *Penninsula* (2020), *Hellbound* sampled many genres: zombie films, social satire, disaster films, and family drama. But unlike the striking reversal of characters and stylistic diversity in *Squid Game*, *Hellbound* came across as much more monotonous due to its sustained hysteria and ludicrous computer-generated effects. Nonetheless, it presented a refreshing take on the millennia-old fear of apocalyptic judgment, recasting it in the mold of abusive media practices that can exact a ruinous toll on society.

It is too early to determine whether recent K-drama sensations such as *Squid Game*, *My Name*, and *Hellbound* collectively speak to audiences' new tastes and needs of the postpandemic streaming era. But the heat is on for sure, with Disney+ and Apple TV increasing their investment in Korean talent and Korean-themed dramas for their platforms. With gripping new commissions such as *Moving*, *Grid*, and *Big Bet* (Disney+), *Dr. Brain* and *Pachinko* (Apple TV), these companies are eager to outdo the unprecedented success of *Squid Game*. To borrow media critic Jason Jeong's words, these recent dramas on streaming sites are "stylistically striking and socially aware," and "they represent a departure from traditional network television."[5]

Romantic comedies and feel-good family dramas still prevail on domestic broadcasting networks, amid growing efforts to diversify the genre conventions. *Squid Game* may be the most dazzling accomplishment in the recent cohort of popular K-drama, the broader Korean drama scene is hardly *Squid Game* writ large. But one common gene seems to tie these recent hits on global streaming to the previous generations of romantic comedy and historical costume drama that enjoyed wide popularity throughout Asia. K-dramas are panegyrics to effusive human emotion—but it's not just individual emotions that scatter in all directions. Most of the shows feature characters with an earnest desire to feel what others feel and act upon those feelings. Whether characters wear green track suits or priest's robes, whether the action takes place on a mystery island or palace grounds, the common thread is a deep plunge into the psychological maze that eventually becomes externalized as the desire to live meaningfully. No emotion is held at bay in searching for all possible means to live as a harmonious collective.

Korea's modern history itself is directly accountable for this cultural DNA. Born of calamity and crisis, in the past two centuries Korea has existed on the scorched grounds of endless foreign invasions, colonization, civil war, and lingering partition. But what remained in the ashes was an inviolable dream of a better life: instead of internalizing victimhood, the wronged longed for a just society. Although such dreams are impossible to realize in the actual world, Korean popular culture turned them into its own bloodstream and heartbeat. It is this surge of desire to realize the impossible that transforms the national particulars into globally shared aspirations. The hopeful visions of the underdog persevere and succeed, knowing no national borders.

The dream of a livable society for all emerges ever more pressingly in trying times, and artists such as Bong Joon-ho and Lee Isaac Chung have captured the present desire to hope against hope, dream against dreams. Just think of Bong's *Parasite* (2019). The Oscar-winning film captures the ambivalent mix of hope, despair, and the futility of dreaming of change that will never be. The film returns to the semibasement where it all started, but this time, Gi-woo is writing a letter to his father that will perhaps never be delivered. At the beginning of the film, his father was in the semibasement dreaming of a better tomorrow, but by the end he has sunk lower into the abyss as an underground fugitive, hunted for his crime. Gi-woo nonetheless does not give up hope of reuniting with his father and ends his letter "until then, good-bye"—an expression of a faint dream that he knows will most likely be unrealized. Chung's *Minari* (2020), a heartfelt Korean American family chronicle of settling in the desolate Arkansas farmland, also concludes with the possibility of making remote dreams come true while bleak reality looms large on the horizon. Although some pure cinephiles will hardly admit these auteur films' kinship with what they see as vapid TV shows, I see how much of their soul is shared with *Squid Game*: the hope of doing good, the endless struggle to get there, and the earnest sharing of life journeys too often derailed.

Such is the prevailing vision that made K-pop supergroup BTS a face of their generation. The recent success of Korean storytelling in the United States comes against the backdrop of the increasing wealth gap, racial violence, and the ensuing social justice movement. BTS's rise to the top of the Billboard charts merged with the explosion of the #MeToo movement, #BlackLivesMatter, and #StopAsianHate. The septet's affirmative impact on the world and their ability to give voice to the voiceless made them truly stand out in Korea's talent-saturated music market. No doubt they regaled the world with their amicable personalities and expert performances, but what made BTS the "it" band of the era is their ability to reflect deeply on the precarity of life.

Underdogs eventually can accrue enough power to shift the rules of the game. To be sure, the success of BTS on a global scale changed the Billboard and MTV playbooks in a substantial way. As K-pop now represents one of the major streams of the global pop music scene, the MTV Video Music Awards in 2019 added a K-pop video award category. To deepen entanglements between the Korean music industry and the global industry, K-pop behemoths BlackPink and NTC127 signed with Interscope Records in 2018 and Capitol Records in 2019, respectively. Joining such moves to procure a launching pad to have their music heard globally is NCT Hollywood auditions, co-organized by MGM and NCT's management company, SM Entertainment, to cultivate a truly local Hollywood group to debut in the United States. BTS's management company, HYBE (formerly Big Hit Entertainment), went beyond a simple partnership. In 2021 HYBE announced that it would create a joint label and groom new K-pop groups based in North America in collaboration with Geffen Records, a subsidiary of the world's largest record label, Universal Music Group. Once having aspired to global stardom, K-pop now seems to be setting the standard for the next generation of global idols.

The most significant change in media relations in the Korean entertainment world was the 2019 opening of Weverse by HYBE. A streaming platform for multimedia content and an artist-to-fan communication platform using mobile apps and websites, Weverse intends to streamline BTS-related content, which previously generated millions of views and retweets on YouTube, Twitter, and TikTok. This is a significant leap forward to claim ownership of its own content distribution—a move that allows the group freedom to shape their own channels of communication. The strategy is many strides ahead of the production model of *Squid Game*, where the Korean production company worked as a de facto subcontractor for the global streaming giant Netflix. The sustained success of BTS and other K-pop groups is definitely changing the music industry, but will such trends apply to the world of drama production as well? Just as K-pop reached the world audience via YouTube, K-drama needs Netflix, Amazon Prime, Disney+, and Apple TV to become a global sensation.

To be sure, there are already the K-drama versions of Weverse: Kokowa and TVING, a Los Angeles–based streaming site, it launched in 2017 to specialize in South Korean dramas, films, docuseries, and variety shows produced by South Korea's three leading networks, MBC,

KBS, and SBS. Kokowa's service model emulates much of what Netflix is already doing: genre-specific categorization, new releases, trending notices, and recommendations. On the other hand, TVING, a joint venture established in 2020 by Korea's major media companies CJ ENM, Naver, and JTBC, streams K-dramas, variety shows, and television films, with hopes of edging out global competitors in K-contents streaming wars. The emergence of Korean drama-specific streaming sites is indicative of the size and impact of the genre outside Korea. It is everyone's dream to be in control of their own destiny, but we will have to see if Weverse, TVING, or Kokowa, mostly focused on Korean content, can sustain viable competition with their global counterparts that omnivorously produce and stream everything.

Inundated with information, we live in an era where even the most gleaming vision soon turns into an outdated spectacle. But some Korean dramas, pop music, and films have emerged as lingering echoes of our times. Some thirty years ago, their worldwide reach was unimaginable, but today, it is difficult to imagine a pop culture world without them. Inching closer and closer to center stage, K-culture exceeds the geopolitical realities of Korea as a nation-state, with all its fantastic visions of what the world could be.

Netflix wants to make sure that *Squid Game* is set to achieve precisely that goal of being indispensable in today's media world. To that effect, on June 12, 2022, Hwang Dong-hyuk dropped a suspenseful announcement about what to expect for the second season of the show.

A WHOLE NEW ROUND IS COMING

It took 12 years to bring the first season of
"Squid Game" to life last year.
But it took 12 days for "Squid Game" to become
The most popular Netflix series ever.

As the writer, director and producer of "Squid Game,"
A huge shout out to fans around the world.
Thank you for watching and loving our show.

And now, Gi-hun returns.
The Front Man returns.
Season 2 is coming.
The man in the suit with ddakji might be back.
You'll also be introduced to Young-hee's boyfriend, Cheol-su.
Join us once more for a whole new round.

Hwang Dong-hyuk
Director, Writer and Executive Producer
of *Squid Game*

In the world of constant stimulation and instant gratification, one cannot be gone from the limelight for too long. Before oblivion sets in, you have to make an announcement that you are still in the game. The grand architect of the gaming arena and its faithful sponsor are once again playing each other's *gganbu*.

Are you in? Ready. Set. Go.

A reset button has been pushed.

The second round of games has begun.

NOTES

INTRODUCTION: LOCAL ARENA FOR GLOBAL GAMES

1. "Director Hwang Comments on *Squid Game*'s Success," *KBS News Line*, December 27, 2021, accessed on December 27, 2021, https://www.youtube.com/watch?v=46kuX02LV1M.

2. Kyung-Sup Chang, "Compressed Modernity and Its Discontents: South Korean Society in Transition," *Economy and Society* 28, no. 1 (February 1999): 31.

3. "*Squid Game* Season 2: HoYeon Jung & Park Hae Soo on Possible Returns," *ExtraTV*, November 9, 2021, accessed on November 9, 2021, https://www.youtube.com/watch?v=t-TH1iwYaM8.

4. "Hot & New Korean TV Shows," *Variety*, accessed on November 12, 2021.

5. "Rapid Rise of K-dramas," YTN News, November 14, 2021, accessed on November 14, 2021, https://www.youtube.com/watch?v=Bhs2Y6p0TeM.

6. Korea Communications Standards Commission, "Announcement on Broadcast Programs (Bangsongpeurogeuraem deungui pyeonseonge gwanhan gosi 2010.2.3.)," February 3, 2010, accessed on October 3, 2022, https://www.law.go.kr/admRulInfoP.do?admRulSeq=2000000013005.

7. Reed Hastings and Erin Meyer, *No Rules Rules* (London: Ebury, 2020).

8. Michael Liedtke, "Netflix Raising Prices for 58M US Subscribers as Costs Rise," AP News, January 15, 2019, assessed on October 2, 2021, https://apnews.com/article/entertainment-north-america-technology-business-ap-top-news-76214d0d5b1a4d0890a2d3040a3ddb33.

9. Reed Hastings, "Consumer Technology Association Keynote 2016," Consumer Electronics Show, accessed on November 11, 2021, www.youtube.com/watch?v=l5R3E6jsICA.

10. Ramon Lobato, *Netflix Nations: The Geography of Digital Distribution* (New York: New York University Press, 2019).

11. Timothy Havens, "Netflix: Streaming Channel Brands as Global Meaning System," in *From Networks to*

Netflix: A Guide to Changing Channels, ed. Derek Johnson (New York: Routledge, 2018), Kindle edition.

12. Panel discussion at "Transforming Hollywood: U.S. Streaming and International Co-productions," December 3, 2021, UCLA.

13. Panel discussion, December 3, 2021, UCLA.

14. "Netflix Celebrates Great Films, Filmmakers and Emerging Talent at the Lumiere Festival," *Netflix News*, October 9, 2021, accessed on October 9, 2021, https://about.netflix.com/en/news/netflix-celebrates-great-films-filmmakers-and-emerging-talent-at-the-lumiere.

15. "*Squid Game*: Hwang Dong-hyuk and Bong Joon-ho in Conversation," *Still Watching Netflix*, June 2, 2022, accessed on June 2, 2022, https://www.youtube.com/watch?v=-d1rZdRnne4.

16. "Rapid Rise of K-dramas."

17. Panel discussion, December 3, 2021, UCLA.

18. Lobato, *Netflix Nations*.

19. "Netflix CEO Reed Hastings Talks Streaming Wars," *New York Times Events*, November 6, 2019, accessed on November 6, 2019, https://www.youtube.com/watch?v=7V6FFeZdFz4.

20. Panel discussion, December 3, 2021, UCLA.

21. According to the *New York Times* report, Netflix told its employees that it could introduce "its lower-priced ad-supported tier by the end of the year, a more accelerated timeline than originally indicated, the company told employees in a recent note." According to the report, the company lost two hundred thousand subscribers in the first three months of 2022, which was the first time that has happened in a decade, and the introduction of the advertisement will mitigate its financial woes. John Koblin and Nicole Sperling, "Netflix Tells Employees Ads May Come by the End of 2022," *New York Times*, May 10, 2022, accessed on May 10, 2022, https://www.nytimes.com/2022/05/10/business/media/netflix-commercials.html.

22. Panel discussion, December 3, 2021, UCLA.

23. Patrick Brzeski, "Netflix to Produce Korean Remake of Hit Spanish Series 'Money Heist,'" *Hollywood Reporter*, November 30, 2020, accessed on November 30, 2021, https://www.hollywoodreporter.com/tv/tv-news/netflix-to-produce-korean-remake-of-hit-spanish-series-money-heist-4098639/.

24. "Netflix CEO Reed Hastings Talks Streaming Wars."

25. James Poniewozik, Mike Hale, and Margaret Lyons, "Best TV Shows of 2020," *New York Times,* December 1, 2020.

26. *Guerilla-casting* is a term I coined to reference the YouTube and social media content produced and shared by individual users. The term designates the phase that follows the microcasting model of internet-age communication, which itself followed broadcasting by the terrestrial TV stations and narrowcasting by the cable TV stations.

27. Hastings, "Consumer Technology Association Annual Meeting Keynote 2016."

28. Julia Stoll, "Most Expensive Netflix Original Series as of March 2021, by Production Cost per Episode," *Statista*, May 19, 2022, accessed on February 22, 2022, https://www.statista.com/statistics/1249573/most-expensive-netflix-original-series-production-cost-per-episode/.

29. Kim Eun-gyeong, "Netflix and the Subordination of Korean Culture," *Dailian*, November 6, 2021, accessed on November 6, 2021, https://news.v.daum.net/v/20211106060000476.

30. Panel discussion, December 3, 2021, UCLA.

31. Patrick Frater, "Netflix under Pressure in Korea as *Squid Game* Success Stirs Lawmakers and Internet Firms," *Variety*, November 3, 2021, accessed on November 3, 2021, https://variety.com/2021/biz/asia/netflix-under-pressure-in-korea-1235104596/.

32. Frater, "Netflix Under Pressure in Korea."

33. Reed Hastings, quoted in Murtuza Ambawala, "Netflix Organizational Culture," accessed on January 13, 2022, https://www.youtube.com/watch?v=7O87hhyLa9U.

34. Kang Hyun-kyung, "*Squid Game* Team Gets Bonus from Netflix," *Korea Times*, November 23, 2021, accessed on November 24, 2021, https://www.koreatimes.co.kr /www/art/2021/11/688_319298.html.

CHAPTER 1. LET THE GAMES BEGIN

1. Lee Ju-hyun, "Lee Jung-jae Says That Immersion into the Fantasy World Was the Key," *Cine21*, September 28, 2021, accessed on October 7, 2022, http://m.cine21.com /news/view/?mag_id=98654.

2. Kim Hyo-eun, "Interview with Hwang Dong-hyuk: I Put Everything in Line Shooting Fortress," *Joongang Ilbo*, October 10, 2017, accessed on October 7, 2022, https:// www.joongang.co.kr/article/21998920#home.

3. Kim, "Interview with Hwang Dong-hyuk."

4. Kim, "Interview with Hwang Dong-hyuk."

5. Kim, "Interview with Hwang Dong-hyuk."

6. Yi Hwa-jeong, "Director Hwang Shares the Film-ing Process of *The Fortress*," *Cine 21*, September 25, 2017,

accessed on October 8, 2022, http://www.cine21.com /news/view/?mag_id=88295.

7. Chae Kyoung-sun, "Global TV: *Squid Game*," Carsey Wolf Center at UCSB, May 12, 2022.

8. Chae Kyoung-sun, Zoom interview with the author, May 31, 2022.

9. Chae, Zoom interview with the author.

10. Chae, "Global TV: *Squid Game*."

11. "*Squid Game*: Hwang Dong-hyuk and Bong Joon-ho in Conversation."

12. Chae, "Global TV: *Squid Game*."

13. Chae, Zoom interview with the author.

14. "*Squid Game*: Hwang Dong-hyuk and Bong Joon-ho in Conversation."

15. "Jung Jae-il according to Bong Jun-ho," JTBC Entertainment, February 2019, accessed on October 22, 2021, https://www.youtube.com/watch?v=WMh7hGlkNzw.

16. "Jung Jae-il according to Bong Jun-ho."

17. "*Squid Game*: Hwang Dong-hyuk and Bong Joon-ho in Conversation."

18. Kim Jeong-yeon, "Jung Jae-il Composes *Squid Game* Music with Drums and Recorders," *Joongang Ilbo*, September 30, 2021, accessed on October 10, 2021, https://www .joongang.co.kr/article/25011230#home.

19. "*Squid Game* OST: Pink Soldiers," *Funky Cats*, September 25, 2021, accessed on October 12, 2022, https://www.youtube.com/watch?v=v9NQYKv2rTg.

CHAPTER 2. PLAY AT YOUR OWN RISK

1. YouTuber Tuff Specialist criticized the long slow motion of the shattering bridge scene as an unnecessary exaggeration: "Do we really need fifty-four seconds of unbroken slow mo for three identical cuts on characters' cheeks? This scene represents so much of what I think holds *Squid Game* back." Tuff Specialist, "Why *Squid Game* Is Overrated," October 2, 2021, accessed March 1, 2022, https://www.youtube.com/watch?v=UIJA1paIRkE. Taking such a view misses the metaphor of a bomb, where the moment of explosion seems to be suspended in apocalyptic time.

2. Beatrice Verhoeven, "*Squid Game*'s Creator Hwang Dong-hyuk Looks Back on Developing the Series," *Hollywood Reporter*, November 19, 2021 accessed November 19, 2021, https://www.hollywoodreporter.com/tv/tv-features/squid-game-creator-hwang-dong-hyuk-series-development-1235049995/.

3. Bill Irwin, UCSB Michael Douglass Lecture, Hatlen Theater, February 18, 2009.

4. Verhoeven, "*Squid Game* Creator Hwang Dong-hyuk Looks Back on Developing the Series."

5. "Director of *Squid Game* Talks about the Hit Show," *Good Morning America*, October 15, 2021, accessed October 15, 2021, https://www.youtube.com/watch?v=-hW_fh0g7c8.

6. Jacques Rancière, *The Philosopher and His Poor*, trans. John Drury, Corinne Oster, and Andrew Parker (Durham, NC: Duke University Press, 2003).

CHAPTER 3. PAINT YOUR DREAMS WITH BLOOD

1. "Director of *Squid Game* Talks about the Hit Show."

2. Chae, Zoom interview with the author.

3. M. C. Escher, *Escher on Escher: Exploring the Infinate* (New York: Abrams, 1989), 76.

4. Escher, *Escher on Escher*, 68.

5. Chae, Zoom interview with the author.

6. "*Squid Game*: Hwang Dong-hyuk and Bong Joon-ho in Conversation."

7. Patty Gone, notes to the author on an earlier version of this chapter.

8. Kim Jung-yeon, "500kg Piggy Bank, Coffin with Pink Ribbon, and Depicting Death Game as Children's

Fairytale," *Joongang Ilbo*, October 3, 2021, accessed on October 5, 2021, https://www.4flix.co.kr/board/info/9308?sca=.

9. Harry Torczyner, *Magritte: Ideas and Images* (New York: Abrams, 1977), 277.

10. Wendy James, quoted in Lewis Hyde, *The Gift: Creativity and the Artist in the Modern World* (New York: Vintage, 2007), 4.

11. Jacques Derrida, *The Gift of Death*, trans. Davis Wills (Chicago: University of Chicago Press, 2008).

12. Hyde, *The Gift,* xvi.

13. "Why Study the Gift with John Milbank," University of Nottingham, March 4, 2015, accessed on March 21, 2022, https://www.youtube.com/watch?v=JvQZf0egisE.

14. Chae, Zoom interview with the author.

15. Chae, Zoom interview with the author.

CODA: THE STAKES OF THE GAME

1. "Squid Game: Tempered Glass vs. Ordinary," SPG Blog, October 19, 2021, accessed on October 20, 2021, https://www.specialistglass.co.uk/squid-game-tempered -glass-vs-ordinary/.

2. "Season 2? Behind the Scenes of *Squid Game* according to Lee Jung-jae," Artist Company, November 8, 2021,

accessed March 25, 2022, https://www.youtube.com/watch?v=hClBJTjk570.

3. On November 3, 2021, Netflix also added three previous films by director Hwang Dong-hyuk. Jacob Siegal, "Netflix Just Added 3 Movies from the Creator of *Squid Game*," BGR, November 3, 2021, accessed on November 3, 2021, https://bgr.com/entertainment/netflix-just-added-3-movies-from-the-creator-of-squid-game/.

4. Hastings, "Consumer Technology Association Keynote 2016."

5. Jason Jeong, "Korean Television Is in the Midst of a Radical Renaissance," *Jacobin*, March 18, 2022, accessed on June 26, 2022, https://jacobin.com/2022/03/radical-renaissance-contemporary-korean-television-violence-neoliberalism.